Sponge Cake

Makes one 9-inch cake

1 cup cake flour (sifted)
1/2 teaspoon baking powder
1/4 t. salt
3 eggs at room temperature (separated
2/3 cup sugar
1 tbl. grated orange rind or
1 teaspoon grated lemon rind
1/4 cup fresh orange juice or a
   To cup water, plus 1 teaspoon vanill
   heat oven to 350°. Lightly grease th
                                9 inch cake pan

small
sweet
treats

MARGUERITE MARCEAU
HENDERSON

photographs by
ZAC WILLIAMS

GIBBS SMITH
TO ENRICH AND INSPIRE HUMANKIND

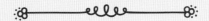

First Edition
15 14 13 12 11   5 4 3 2 1

Text © 2011 Marguerite Marceau Henderson
Photographs © 2011 Zac Williams

Published by
Gibbs Smith
P.O. Box 667
Layton, Utah 84041

1.800.835.4993 orders
www.gibbs-smith.com

Designed by Alison Oliver
Printed and bound in Hong Kong

Gibbs Smith books are printed on paper produced from sustainable PEFC-
certified forest/controlled wood source. Learn more at www.pefc.org.

Library of Congress Cataloging-in-Publication Data

Henderson, Marguerite Marceau.
Small sweet treats / Marguerite Marceau Henderson ;
photographs by Zac Williams. — 1st ed.
p. cm.
ISBN 978-1-4236-0694-9
1. Desserts. 2. Pastry. 3. Cookbooks. I. Williams, Zac. II. Title.
TX773.H379 2011
641.8'6—dc22
2011006573

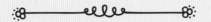

This cookbook is dedicated to my late mother,
Rose Marceau (1915–2001), my kitchen muse.
Her dedication to and love of her family, her
inspiration at the stove, and her genteel nature
have provided fond memories for her two
children, four grandchildren, and the future
generation of great-grandchildren.

Contents

Acknowledgments

ALMOST IMMEDIATELY AFTER my third cookbook, *Small Parties,* was released, my editor, Jennifer Adams, called me to ask, "And, so what shall we do for your next book?"

I had barely recuperated from the whirlwind book signings of *Parties,* and here we were contemplating another book. What was left in the series of *Small* titles? Desserts, why of course!

Now, I love desserts. I am a lemon person. Chocolate is nice, but creamy lemon is better. But an entire book of desserts was daunting to me. Over 100 recipes. I could do it, but it would require hours of recipe development and evaluating. Recipes that needed to be precise. Nothing left to chance. No improvisations here.

The testing began. My next-door neighbors, Mary and Jim Schwing, were often presented with four to five different sweets at once. My friends and the baristas at the neighborhood Starbucks were bestowed with plates of tested delights every Sunday. The treats were rated. Notes were taken. Waistlines expanded.

Friends were invited to sample not one, but sometimes two, three, or four desserts after my abundant Italian meals. More waistlines expanded. I gave parties with the excuse to showcase another sweet recipe or two. And when asked to bring something to a gathering or a dinner, the host or hostess would preface it by saying something to the effect of, "How about bringing a dessert? I

know you are testing recipes and we would love to be part of the process."

In many of my cooking classes, desserts were highlighted. Hundreds of students over the past two years have appreciated being test guinea pigs, I think!

And, honestly, there were days when I had so many goodies coming out of the oven, displayed on the counter and on platters, that I posted an invitation to friends on Facebook to please come by and relieve me of the copious amounts of sweet treats. And come they did. At all hours of the night.

I have so many people to thank in my culinary world. First and foremost, my immediate family: my son, Justin Henderson, and my daughter, Sarah Henderson Collins, and their spouses, Heather and Sean. They have lived with my crazy cooking class schedules and my obsession with entertaining with not one, two, or three courses, but at least four or five, and they love my visits when their kitchens have been commandeered by my whirling dirvish dinner preparations. Their friends look forward to my visits, too!

And lately, my twin granddaughters, Gianna and Lillian, consider me their personal baker. "Let's make cookies, Mimi." "Brown cupcakes, Mimi . . . with sparkles, please." I am always preheating the oven for any request at any time. Halloween cookies, painted with orange frosting and decorated with black, yellow, white, and orange sprinkles. Aebleskivers for breakfast, filled with raspberry jam and chocolate chips, floating in pure maple syrup.

Good cooks run in the family. My daughter, son, son-in-law, and daughter-in-law are fine cooks and bakers. My brother holds his own, entertaining dozens of family members and friends, and my cousins and their spouses in New York also carry on the family tradition of cooking for large groups.

My late mother, Rose Marceau, was a baker and a cook extraordinaire in her own right. Almost no recipe of Craig Claiborne's from *The New York Times* in the 1960s went untested in her kitchen. She was the first person I knew who studied and cooked from Julia Child's *The Art of French Cooking, Volumes 1 and 2* before it became fashionable. She baked cookies, cream puffs, and cakes and created Italian Christmas dolci that would humble most Food Network stars. She was my inspiration. She is my muse. She was a classic "grandma" who made my children after-school delights they recall to this day, from rice pudding to carrot layer cake.

Thank-you to my students who give me such pleasure in my profession, and to my wealth of friends who give encouragement to follow my culinary dreams. A special thank-you to my kitchen assistants, Mary, Kristin, and Mary Martha who, for the love of food, contributed to the photo shoots of my last three books and keep my kitchen organized during classes.

And thanks to my dear, dear friends all around the country who tolerate the photographing of each plate when dining out, as well as stopping at every farmers market within a ten-mile radius to photograph and taste more. They also put up with eating in as many establishments as one person could muster the energy and appetite to do—tasting morning pastries to local cheeses and wines, food cart delicacies, happy-hour appetizers, decadent desserts, specialty coffees, and anything else the region might have to offer. We eat, drink, laugh, and walk—miles and miles.

And I would like to say thank-you to Charlotte Christensen. She is a dear friend who lived on bucolic Whidbey Island, who invited me to visit last fall and lodge in a home where I worked feverishly for five days on this book, while overlooking Penn Cove. Charlotte and her husband, Maury, were so gracious in providing me with solitude during the day, but companionship, many spirits, and nourishment in the evenings. Charlotte passed away unexpectedly this past December 2010, and life without her on Whidbey Island will never be the same. But her culinary spirit remains. Thank you, Charlotte. We shared many memorable meals, martinis, laughs, and heartaches.

I hope, in some minute way, I have put smiles on faces, joy in hearts, and warmth in tummies. My legacy in this world.

Introduction

ON HER MOST RECENT VISIT, my daughter Sarah, now a mother of four-year-old twin girls, walked through my front door, stopped, and declared, "I am home!" She was not just reentering the house in which she was brought up, but smelling two loaves of banana-pecan-coconut bread baking in the oven. Her memories of a food-filled kitchen returned with the simple aroma of warm banana bread.

I decided to make that particular sweet delight because I thought a few loaves of bread, requiring mere minutes of preparation time, would bring joy to guests in my kitchen. Fortunately, a bunch of bananas bought days earlier were turning darker and softer than I prefer to eat with my morning cereal. And the loaves performed beautifully. While they were cooling on baking racks, Sarah eagerly inquired when one would be cool enough to slice and top with butter.

This is what I hope to convey to readers of this cookbook: the joy of simple, sweet treats that can be made in every kitchen. You will discover that any kitchen can be the place where a family reminisces about an intensely rich chocolate pudding cake emerging from the oven, zesty Meyer lemon custard simmering on the cooktop, or dark chocolate chip–walnut cookie dough mixed and ready to be scooped onto baking sheets.

You have those food memories already, and they are probably about decadent treats.

That perfect apple pie Grandma used to bake with a crust made with lard and love? The dark chocolate tilted layer cake Mother created for every birthday, spread thick with buttercream and decorated with colored sprinkles and dragées?

One of my favorite food recollections is of a New York egg cream. It's a beverage that has neither eggs nor cream, but the nostalgia of sitting up to a classic Brooklyn "soda fountain" and ordering a cold egg cream lingers. I decided to expand on tradition and created the Egg Cream Float by adding ice cream, making it more substantial, yet keeping the integrity of the drink.

In addition to the joy of sweet treats, I also want readers to observe that small, edible pleasures, mere indulgences, should be just that—a luxurious bite that satisfies sensually for a few moments. A treat after being scrupulous during the day, and through dinner, in the anticipation of a final reward. Then, the pleasure from that bite—of, say, a nut cake dripping with toffee sauce—will linger in your food memory for hours, days, weeks, and years.

I wrote this book to give readers a chance to create their own joyous food memories. It was not without trepidation, I must admit, and not just because the subject—the sweet bite—was something that takes time to prepare. More than the time involved, desserts require implements such as

measuring spoons, measuring cups, rolling pins, proper pans, and a timer.

My cooking class students know me as one who doesn't measure. After thirty years of teaching, I impart my love of food to the students by giving recipes to use as springboards, starting points. Use the basic recipe and change to your tastes. I hardly ever measure when creating savory dishes. I use my culinary sense and kitchen experience as to which ingredients to add, delete, or multiply. That's how I cook.

Not so with baking. It's a science. It's about precision and following directions as written, for fear of a flat cake or a cookie with no taste. My advice for users of this book is to follow these recipes as written. They have been tested, retested, and then created again for the photo shoot.

Fresh fruits. Dried fruits. Nuts. Citrus. Chocolate. Spices. All these combine to create lingering aromas, tastes, and nostalgia for long-ago kitchen experiences. With fastidious attention, they can also combine to create a breakfast masterpiece like the Real Deal New York Crumb Cake. Followed faithfully, that recipe provides a moist yellow cake base, and a respectable thickness of cinnamon-scented buttery crumbs, with a dusting of powdered sugar. The result is a weekend must-have that we New Yorkers take with a cup of "regular."

Like the crumb cake, the other recipes in this book are ready for preparation in your kitchen. The kitchen is the heart of your home, the place where your family's best moments are made. And your family will long for and fondly remember the process of making these treats. The perfumed aroma of sugar and spice in a mixing bowl ready for transformation into a cupcake. The afternoon spent decorating orange cardamom buttons. The feel of the pastry bag filling Sicilian cannoli.

True, delicious pastries are a reward for the flour-covered floors, sticky countertops, and cream-covered bowls. But your kitchen will be treasured and beloved for all the joy that went into making those small, sweet treats.

FILL THAT
COOKIE JAR

pistachio-lemon-lavender shortbread cookies

Nuts, citrus, and a floral herb create a most aromatic cookie. Tea, anyone?

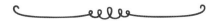

1/3 cup sugar

1 teaspoon culinary lavender buds

1 teaspoon finely grated lemon zest

2 tablespoons lemon juice

1/2 cup unsalted butter, softened

1 1/4 cups all-purpose flour

1/4 cup finely chopped pistachio nuts

1/2 teaspoon kosher salt

1/4 cup finely chopped pistachio nuts

2 to 3 tablespoons turbinado (raw sugar) or sanding sugar

In a mixer bowl, beat the sugar, lavender, lemon zest, lemon juice, and butter until fluffy, about 30 seconds, using the paddle attachment. Slowly beat in the flour, 1/4 cup pistachios, and salt, beating until a soft dough forms, about 1 minute on medium speed.

Transfer dough to a floured board; divide in half and roll each half into logs that are about 1- x 10-inches long. Spread the remaining pistachios onto floured board. Roll each log in the nuts. Wrap each log in plastic wrap and chill for 1 hour. (Dough can also be frozen for up to 1 month.) Slice the shortbread dough into 1/4-inch-thick rounds. Place on parchment-lined baking sheets. Sprinkle lightly with sugar. Bake on the middle rack of a 350-degree-F oven for 15 to 20 minutes, until edges are just turning golden brown. Transfer to wire rack to cool.

Makes about 4 dozen cookies.

double dark chocolate cherry cookies

Do you love German Black Forest cake? This double chocolate cookie base with dried cherries will definitely satisfy your taste buds.

½ cup unsalted butter, softened

⅓ cup brown sugar

⅔ cup sugar

2 large eggs

2 teaspoons vanilla extract

¼ cup cocoa powder

½ teaspoon kosher salt

1¼ cups all-purpose flour

½ teaspoon baking soda

1 cup extra dark chocolate chips (Guittard's 63 percent cacao)

1 cup dried cherries, finely chopped

Pink sprinkles or sanding sugar

In the bowl of a mixer, beat the butter with the sugars with the paddle attachment until light yellow and fluffy. Beat in the eggs, vanilla, cocoa, salt, flour, and baking soda until well combined. Add the chocolate chips and cherries, beating until the dough forms a solid ball.

With a 1-inch diameter ice cream scoop, form balls of dough, and place them 2 inches apart on baking sheets lined with parchment paper or Silpat. Sprinkle each ball of dough with pink sprinkles or sanding sugar. Bake on the middle rack of a preheated 375-degree-F oven for 15 minutes, until cookies have puffed; cool slightly. *Makes about 20 to 22 cookies.*

almond tuiles

Tuiles, meaning "tiles" in French, are the ideal little vessels
for berries, ice cream, mousse, or even as a garnish for your bowl
of berries, pudding, or ice cream. Silpat or parchment paper lining
for the baking sheets is a must to prevent sticking.

½   cup finely ground almonds

¼   cup all-purpose flour

½   cup sugar

¼   teaspoon kosher salt

2   large egg whites

5   tablespoons unsalted
    butter, melted

¼   teaspoon almond extract

²/₃ cup slightly toasted
     sliced almonds

In a mixing bowl, whisk the ground almonds, flour, sugar, and salt. Beat the egg whites in a separate bowl until stiff peaks form. Fold the egg whites, melted butter, and almond extract into the dry ingredients until well combined. Place Silpat or parchment paper on two baking sheets. Drop rounded teaspoons of the batter onto the prepared baking sheets about 4 inches apart, spreading out the batter with the back of the spoon to a 3-inch round. Sprinkle a few sliced almonds on each cookie. There will only be 4 cookies per baking sheet.

Bake on the middle rack of a preheated 325-degree-F oven for about 8 minutes until light brown. Working quickly, remove cookies from baking sheet and drape over a rolling pin or place over an inverted glass to form a "cup." (If the cookies become too brittle to form, return to baking sheet and into oven for a few seconds to allow cookies to soften.) Cool completely before removing cookies from inverted glass. Continue to make the tuiles in this manner with remaining batter. *Makes about 16 cookies.*

almond biscotti

Your kitchen will possess the aroma of an Italian bakery in Little Italy
when you makes these cookies. The almonds combined with vanilla
slowly baking in your oven will attract neighbors far and wide.
These biscottis are delicious, dipped into coffee or tea. Buon appetito!

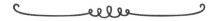

1   cup sliced or whole
    almonds, slightly
    toasted*

2   cups all-purpose flour

3/4   cup sugar

1/2   cup unsalted butter,
    room temperature

2   large eggs

1/2   teaspoon kosher salt

1   teaspoon baking powder

1   teaspoon vanilla extract

1   egg beaten with
    1 tablespoon cream
    (egg wash)

In a food processor, coarsely chop the almonds. Add
the flour, sugar, butter, eggs, salt, baking powder,
and vanilla. Mix until dough is well combined. Turn
out the dough onto a floured work surface. Divide
in half and roll into logs about 2 inches in diameter.
Place on a parchment- or Silpat-lined baking sheet.
Brush the tops with the egg wash. Bake on the middle
rack of a preheated 250-degree-F oven for 30 to
35 minutes. Remove and cool for 10 minutes. With
a serrated knife, cut into 1-inch-thick slices on the
diagonal. Place the sliced cookies on a wire cookie
rack back on the baking sheet. Bake an additional 10
minutes at 250 degrees F or until crispy. Remove
from oven; cool slightly. *Makes about 20 biscotti.*

**To toast the almonds, place in a skillet over low heat for 3 to
5 minutes, tossing often to prevent the nuts from burning. You
want them just warmed through for a more intense flavor.*

cardamom orange buttons

Little bites scented with cardamom and orange and coated with a light glaze, these cookies accentuate the combination of spice and citrus.

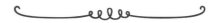

3 ½ cups all-purpose flour

2 ½ teaspoons baking powder

¼ teaspoon kosher salt

3 large eggs

½ cup sugar

½ cup unsalted butter, slightly softened

Finely grated zest of 1 orange

½ teaspoon ground cardamom

½ cup whole milk

2 teaspoons vanilla extract

GLAZE

2 cups powdered sugar

Juice of 1 large orange

Colored candy sprinkles, sanding sugar, or orange sugar dots

In a small bowl, sift the flour and baking powder together.

In a mixing bowl, beat the salt, eggs, and sugar until light and lemon colored, about 2 minutes on medium speed. Add the butter, orange zest, and cardamom. Slowly add the flour mixture, beating on low until combined. Gradually add the milk and vanilla. Dough should be soft. Divide the dough into four sections.

Roll out the dough on a floured work surface to ½ inch thickness. Cut into 1-inch-round buttons with a biscuit cutter. Place on a parchment- or Silpat-lined baking sheet. Bake at 350 degrees F for 10 to 12 minutes until light brown. Do not overbake. Remove from oven and cool.

In a small bowl, whisk the powdered sugar with the orange juice to form a spreading consistency icing. Add a little more juice or a teaspoon of milk to thin, if needed. Brush the tops of each cookie with the glaze, sprinkle with sanding sugar, or use tweezers to place dots (3 to 5) on each. *Makes about 5 dozen cookies.*

anise biscotti

These soft biscotti are perfect with coffee, tea, or a tall
glass of cold milk, as dipping is imperative.

2 large eggs

¼ cup sugar

1 tablespoon honey

2 teaspoons anise extract

1 cup all-purpose flour

½ teaspoon baking powder

In a mixer bowl, beat the eggs and sugar for 3 to 4
minutes on medium speed until doubled in volume
and light yellow in color. Mix in the honey and anise
extract. Beat for another 20 seconds.

In another bowl, combine the flour and baking
powder. Incorporate the flour mixture into the egg
mixture slowly and mix well. Allow the batter to stand
for 15 to 20 minutes. This step is a must for the
sponge-like texture you want to achieve.

Line a baking sheet with parchment paper. Spread the
batter down the center of the pan to form a log that
is 16 x 3 inches. Bake in a preheated 400-degree-F
oven for 12 to 15 minutes until top is golden brown
and the loaf is firm. Remove from oven and allow to
cool for 10 minutes. With a serrated knife, cut into
¾-inch-wide slices. Cookies should be soft and have
a sponge-like texture. *Makes about 24 cookies.*

hazelnut shortbread nutella sandwich cookies

A celebrated combination of dark chocolate and hazelnuts in a spread—Nutella—is sandwiched between toasted hazelnut cookies. Perfection!

3 cups all-purpose flour

3/4 cup powdered sugar

1/2 cup toasted and coarsely ground hazelnuts

1/4 teaspoon kosher salt

1/2 teaspoon vanilla extract

1 1/4 cups unsalted butter, cut into small pieces

1 cup Nutella

Stir together the flour, sugar, hazelnuts, and salt in a mixer bowl. Add the vanilla and butter and mix until the dough resembles coarse meal. Continue to mix until dough forms a ball and holds together. Remove from bowl. Divide dough into two sections. Roll out the dough on a floured board to a log about 2 inches in diameter. Chill until dough has hardened enough to slice.

Line two baking sheets with parchment paper or Silpat. Cut the dough into $1/8$-inch-thick slices. Place slices on prepared baking sheets. Bake on the middle rack of a 325-degree-F oven for 15 to 18 minutes until golden brown. Remove from oven and cool completely. Spread about 1 teaspoon Nutella on bottom of half of the cookies. Top with the remaining cookies to form sandwiches. *Makes about 16 sandwich cookies.*

french vanilla madeleines

A French delicacy, madeleines personify the perfect "after dinner" or "with coffee" treat. Shaped like a scallop shell, these classic French cookies freeze well, too.

Special equipment:
madeleine molds
(petite or regular)

2 large eggs

1/2 cup sugar

1 teaspoon vanilla extract
or vanilla bean paste

1/8 teaspoon kosher salt

1 cup all-purpose flour

10 tablespoons unsalted
butter, slightly melted

Powdered sugar

Spray the madeleine molds with nonstick cooking spray; set aside.

Using an electric mixer, beat the eggs and sugar until blended, about 2 minutes on medium speed. Beat in the vanilla and salt and slowly add in the flour. Mix on low speed until blended, about 30 seconds. Gradually add the melted butter while beating on low speed for another 30 seconds.

Using a pastry bag or a plastic ziplock bag with the tip of the bag snipped off, pipe batter into molds, about 1 teaspoon per indentation. Bake on the middle rack at 375 degrees F for about 8 minutes, or until puffed and just slightly golden brown. Cool 5 minutes before removing the cookies from the pan. Wash molds, spray again, and repeat process for second batch. Dust the "scallop" side of the cookies with powdered sugar just before serving. *Makes about 60 cookies.*

NOTE: To make a lemon or orange flavor, add 1/2 teaspoon finely grated zest to the batter when adding the butter.

hazelnut lemon crescents

These sweet miniature crescents, dusted with powdered
sugar, are ideal for teas and buffets, or with ice cream.

1 cup unsalted butter,
softened

½ cup powdered sugar

2 cups all-purpose flour

¼ teaspoon baking powder

1 teaspoon vanilla extract

1 teaspoon finely grated
lemon zest

1 cup finely chopped
hazelnuts

2 cups powdered sugar

In a mixer bowl, cream the butter and ½ cup
powdered sugar until creamy, about 2 minutes, at
medium speed. Slowly add the flour, baking powder,
vanilla, lemon zest, and hazelnuts and beat on low
speed for another minute. Dough should be soft.
Shape dough into 1-inch crescents and place on
parchment- or Silpat-lined baking sheets. Bake
on the middle rack of a 325-degree-F oven for
15 minutes or until lightly golden. While still slightly
warm, remove cookies from baking sheet and gently
roll into the 2 cups powdered sugar until coated on
all sides; cool completely. *Makes about 3 dozen cookies.*

italian sandwich cookies with raspberry jam

Just like those found in Italian bakeries, these cookies combine orange and raspberry flavors in one bite.

1 cup powdered sugar

1 cup unsalted butter, softened

3 large eggs

2 1/4 cups all-purpose flour

2 teaspoons dark rum

1 teaspoon vanilla extract

2 teaspoons orange extract

1 cup raspberry jam or preserves

In the bowl of a mixer, cream the powdered sugar and butter together until light in color and fluffy, about 2 minutes, with the paddle attachment. Add the eggs, one at a time, beating well after each addition. Beat in the flour, rum, vanilla, and orange extract. Dough should be manageable at this point.

Line two baking sheets with parchment paper. Using a disposable plastic pastry bag, pipe dough onto baking sheets into 2- x 1/2-inch-wide oval shapes. Try to make the cookies the same size so that they will fit together when making the "sandwiches." Bake for 10 minutes at 350 degrees F. Let cool; spread about 1 teaspoon jam or preserves on the flat side of half of the cookies. Top cookies with remaining halves and press together to make sandwiches. Dust with powdered sugar just before serving. *Makes about 2 dozen sandwiches.*

NOTE: This cookie is traditionally served with one end dipped in chocolate and then into candied sprinkles or sanding sugar. To do this, heat about 4 ounces semisweet chocolate in a double boiler over low heat, and then dip each cookie into the warm chocolate and then into sprinkles or sugar. Cool completely on parchment paper before serving.

mocha latte brownie bites

Chocolate, coffee, walnuts, and white chocolate all combine
to make these a sweet finale. When cut into small triangular bites,
these brownies are ideal for the buffet table.

2 squares (2 ounces)
   unsweetened chocolate

½ cup unsalted butter

2 tablespoons instant
   espresso crystals

2 tablespoons unsweetened
   cocoa powder

2 large eggs

1 cup sugar

2 teaspoons vanilla extract

½ cup all-purpose flour

½ teaspoon kosher salt

¾ cup chopped walnuts

¼ cup white chocolate
   morsels

   Powdered sugar

Place the chocolate and butter in a small saucepan
and heat over low heat, stirring until melted. Add the
instant espresso and cocoa powder; cool slightly.

In a mixer bowl, beat the eggs and sugar until
thickened, about 3 minutes, on medium speed. Stir
in the cooled chocolate mixture and vanilla. Fold in
the flour, salt, walnuts, and white chocolate morsels.

Grease and flour an 8- x 8- x 2-inch baking pan.
Pour the batter into pan. Bake on the middle rack of
a preheated 350-degree-F oven for 22 to 25 minutes
until the brownies are set; cool in pan. With a knife,
loosen the edges of the brownies and turn out onto a
cutting board. Cut into 2-inch squares and then cut
into triangles. Sprinkle with powdered sugar. *Makes 32
brownie triangles.*

nanaimo bars

There's a little community on Vancouver Island called Nanaimo. They have become famous for this luscious creation, designed for those who have a serious sweet tooth.

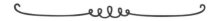

1 cup butter, melted

2/3 cup cocoa powder

1/2 cup sugar

2 eggs, lightly beaten

3 cups graham cracker crumbs

2 cups shredded coconut

1 cup finely chopped walnuts

6 tablespoons unsalted butter, melted

1/4 cup milk

2 teaspoons vanilla extract

4 cups powdered sugar

TOPPING

8 ounces semisweet chocolate morsels

2 tablespoons butter

Grease a 9- x 13-inch metal cake pan and line it with the parchment paper, leaving 1-inch extending over the long edges for handles; set aside.

In a large bowl, whisk together the melted butter, cocoa powder, sugar, and eggs; stir in cracker crumbs, coconut, and walnuts. Press evenly into prepared pan. Bake in center of a 350-degree-F oven for 10 minutes. Let cool in pan on a wire rack.

In a large bowl, stir together the butter, milk, and vanilla; beat in sugar until thickened and smooth. Spread evenly over cooled base. Refrigerate for about 45 minutes or until firm.

Meanwhile, over a pan of hot (not boiling) water, melt the chocolate with the butter. Spread evenly over filling; refrigerate until set. Using parchment paper handles, lift out of pan. Peel off paper and cut into bars. *Makes 24 bars.*

NOTE: These bars can be made ahead. Just cover and store at room temperature for up to 2 days or overwrap with heavy-duty foil and freeze for up to 2 weeks.

oatmeal craisin spicy nut cookies

For a cookie that encompasses all that is yummy in one bite—oatmeal, craisins, nuts, and spices—and still has a chewy texture, try these easy-to-assemble treats. In the fall, you can substitute raisins or dried currants for the craisins, but the little burgundy-hued sweetness of the craisins adds more personality and flavor. Try with dried cherries, too!

1	cup unsalted butter, softened
1¼	cups firmly packed dark brown sugar
½	cup sugar
1¾	cups all-purpose flour
1	teaspoon baking soda
½	teaspoon kosher salt
½	teaspoon ground cinnamon
½	teaspoon ground allspice
2	large eggs
2	teaspoons vanilla extract
2	cups quick-cooking oats
1¼	cups craisins (dried cranberries)
½	cup finely chopped lightly toasted hazelnuts

In the bowl of a mixer, beat the butter and sugars until creamy, about 2 minutes on medium speed.

In another bowl, combine the flour, baking soda, salt, cinnamon, and allspice. Slowly add the dry ingredients to the butter mixture, beating on low speed to incorporate. Add the eggs, vanilla, oats, craisins, and hazelnuts. Beat another 1 to 2 minutes on low speed just until well mixed.

Use a 1-inch ice cream scoop or a tablespoon to place dough 2 inches apart on Silpat- or parchment-lined baking sheets, about 18 cookies per sheet. Bake on the middle rack of a preheated 350-degree-F oven for 10 to 12 minutes. Cookies will be slightly soft in the center. Cool slightly before removing from baking sheet. *Makes about 36 cookies.*

NOTE: These cookies freeze well, too, so bake a batch on Sunday for treats all week long.

oregon hazelnut chocolate chip currant cookies

I love hazelnuts in everything edible from salads to desserts. If you don't have the same passion for this Oregonian export, substitute the hazelnuts with walnuts or pecans. The cookies will still have the same chewy texture.

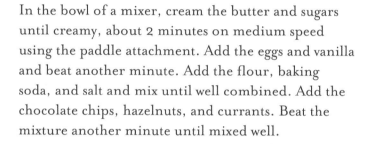

½ cup unsalted butter, softened

⅓ cup sugar

⅓ cup packed dark brown sugar

2 large eggs

1 teaspoon vanilla extract

1½ cups all-purpose flour

½ teaspoon baking soda

¼ teaspoon kosher salt

12 ounces jumbo chocolate chips

½ cup chopped hazelnuts

½ cup dried currants

In the bowl of a mixer, cream the butter and sugars until creamy, about 2 minutes on medium speed using the paddle attachment. Add the eggs and vanilla and beat another minute. Add the flour, baking soda, and salt and mix until well combined. Add the chocolate chips, hazelnuts, and currants. Beat the mixture another minute until mixed well.

Line two baking sheets with parchment paper or Silpat. Use a 1-inch diameter ice cream scoop to form 30 cookies, placing 15 on each baking sheet. Bake the cookies, one tray at a time, on the middle rack of a 350-degree-F oven for 15 minutes. Cookies will be thick and chewy, not thin and crispy. *Makes 2½ dozen cookies.*

peanut butter pecan chocolate chip cookies

A scrumptious combination of peanuts, chocolate, and pecans all fashioned into one bite-sized cookie. Adjust the recipe to your liking and substitute your favorite nuts—such as peanuts, walnuts, or macadamia—for the pecans; substitute white chocolate bits for the semisweet chocolate bits; or use chunky peanut butter instead of creamy.

½ cup unsalted butter, softened

⅓ cup creamy peanut butter

⅓ cup sugar

⅓ cup dark brown sugar

1 large egg

2 teaspoons vanilla extract

¼ teaspoon kosher salt

1¼ cups all-purpose flour

½ teaspoon baking soda

1 cup semisweet chocolate bits

1 cup chopped pecan pieces

½ cup turbinado (raw sugar)

In a mixer bowl, beat the butter, peanut butter, and sugars until fluffy, about 2 minutes on medium speed. Add the egg, vanilla, and salt; mix for 30 seconds. Slowly add the flour and baking soda; beat another minute. Stir in the chocolate and pecans.

Line two large baking sheets with parchment paper. With a 1-inch diameter ice cream scoop, form 30 balls of dough and place 15 on each baking sheet. Press dough down slightly with the bottom of a glass dipped in flour. Sprinkle each cookie with a little raw sugar. Bake on the middle rack of a preheated 350-degree-F oven for 10 to 12 minutes or until golden brown. You might have to bake the sheets of cookies one at a time. Cool slightly before removing from pan. *Makes 30 bite-sized cookies.*

raspberry oatmeal bars

Tart raspberries, topped with a crispy oatmeal crumble and then baked and
cut into bars, can be a perfect picnic treat, a dessert for a potluck dinner,
or just to have handy when unexpected guests make an appearance.

1½ cups all-purpose flour

1 cup firmly packed
   brown sugar

1 cup quick-cooking oats

1 teaspoon ground cinnamon

½ cup unsalted butter, melted

1 tablespoon vanilla extract

12 ounces frozen
    unsweetened
    raspberries, defrosted

   Water

¼ cup sugar

2 teaspoons cornstarch

1 tablespoon water

In a medium bowl, combine the flour, brown sugar,
oats, cinnamon, butter, and vanilla; mix well.

Drain the package of raspberries and reserve the
juice in a small bowl. Add enough water to the
juice to measure ½ cup. Place the raspberry juice
in a small saucepan and bring to a simmer with the
sugar. Dissolve the cornstarch in 1 tablespoon water
in a small bowl; mix well. Add to the raspberry
juice mixture and simmer for 3 to 4 minutes until
thickened. Add raspberries to the liquid in the
saucepan and cook for 2 minutes over medium heat;
cool slightly.

Press two-thirds of the oatmeal mixture in a 9- x
7- x 2-inch baking pan. Spread the raspberry
mixture over the base; top with remaining oatmeal
mixture. Bake on the middle rack of a preheated
350-degree-F oven for 45 minutes. Cool in the
refrigerator for 1 hour before cutting. Serve with ice
cream or whipped cream. *Makes 15 bars.*

pistachio honey rolls

Exotic flavors of honey, pistachios, and cinnamon combine to form a diminutive bite of crunchiness. These do take some time to assemble, but are so worth the final product. When working with phyllo dough, have a damp dish towel handy and work quickly to prevent the dough from drying out. It's a delicate dough, so take care in handling.

2	cups shelled pistachio nuts
½	cup sugar
½	teaspoon ground cinnamon
1	teaspoon finely grated orange zest
16	sheets phyllo dough, rolled out and kept covered with a damp towel
4	tablespoons butter, melted
½	cup honey, warmed

Place the nuts, sugar, cinnamon, and orange zest in a food processor and grind until nuts are finely chopped. Transfer to a bowl.

Place a sheet of phyllo dough on a work surface. Keep the remaining sheets covered with a damp towel after each sheet is used. Brush the sheet of phyllo with butter, top with another sheet of phyllo and brush with more butter. Lightly spread the sheet of phyllo with some of the nut mixture. Cut the phyllo into four strips lengthwise. Roll up each strip, starting at the bottom, and place on a Silpat- or parchment-lined baking sheet, seam side down. Continue with remaining 14 sheets of phyllo and nut filling. Bake on the middle rack of a preheated 375-degree-F oven for 15 minutes. While still warm, drizzle with honey. Allow to cool completely before serving. *Makes 32 rolls.*

umberto cookies

These cookies are found in most Italian pastry shops. They are not too sweet and perfect for serving with cups of espresso or tea. They also store well in airtight containers.

1 cup sugar

6 tablespoons unsalted
   butter, softened

2 large eggs

½ cup whole milk

2 tablespoons honey

2 teaspoons vanilla extract

1 teaspoon lemon extract

5 cups all-purpose flour

2 teaspoons baking soda

2 teaspoons baking powder

1 teaspoon kosher salt

In the bowl of a mixer, cream the sugar and butter until light in color and fluffy, about 2 minutes, with a paddle attachment. Beat in the eggs, milk, honey, vanilla, and lemon extract.

In another bowl, mix the flour, baking soda, baking powder, and salt. Slowly add the flour mixture to the butter mixture, beating well after each addition. The dough should be workable at this point. Add more flour, a few tablespoons at a time, if dough seems too wet.

Sprinkle work surface lightly with flour. Knead the dough into a ball, cut in half and roll out each half to a rectangle shape about ¼ inch thick. Cut the dough into smaller rectangles, about 2- x 3-inches, and place on parchment-lined baking sheets. Keep rolling and cutting dough until all the cookies have been formed. Run the tines of a fork down the tops of each cookie, lengthwise, deep enough to make an indentation. Bake each sheet on the middle rack of a preheated 400-degree-F oven for 10 minutes. Remove from oven and cool until ready to serve.

Makes about 40 cookies.

sesame anise bites

Fragrant seeds of sesame and anise,
make for a delightful tea cookie.

1 cup lightly toasted
   sesame seeds

2 teaspoons anise seeds

1 cup unsalted butter,
   softened

¼ teaspoon baking soda

⅔ cup sugar

2 large egg yolks

1 teaspoon vanilla extract

2½ cups all-purpose flour

1 teaspoon kosher salt

Combine the sesame and anise seeds in a bowl;
set aside.

In a mixer bowl, beat the butter, baking soda, and
sugar until creamy. Add the egg yolks, vanilla, flour,
salt, and seeds. Mix until just combined, about
30 seconds. On a floured board, roll out the dough
and divide into four sections. Roll each section into
4-inch-round discs. Wrap each section of dough in
plastic wrap and chill in the refrigerator for 1 hour.
On a floured board, roll out each section to an
8-inch round. Cut each section into 16 wedges.
Place on a parchment-lined baking sheet. Bake at
350 degrees F for 12 minutes, until just golden.
Makes 64 cookies.

salt and pepper chocolate cookies

Originally a spicy chocolate Mexican cookie, this recipe has been changed to have a more contemporary flair with the addition of sea salt. A bit of heat, cooled with salt—the combination really works.

1 1/2 cups unsalted butter, softened

1 1/3 cups sugar

4 large eggs

3 to 3 1/2 cups all-purpose flour

1 1/2 cups cocoa powder

1/4 teaspoon kosher salt

1/2 teaspoon ground black pepper

1 teaspoon ground cinnamon

1 tablespoon gray sea salt

In a mixer bowl, beat the butter and sugar until light yellow and fluffy, about 2 to 3 minutes on medium speed. Add the eggs, one at a time, and beat another minute.

In a bowl, mix 3 cups flour, cocoa, salt, pepper, and cinnamon. Gradually add to the butter mixture, beating until well blended. If the dough seems to be too soft to work, add a few tablespoons of flour at a time to form a more stiff and workable dough. Divide the dough into fourths. Wrap each section in plastic wrap. Chill for at least 1 hour.

On a floured board, roll out each section of dough to 1/8 inch thickness and cut into desired shapes with cookie cutters. Place on Silpat- or parchment-lined baking sheets. Sprinkle each cookie very lightly with the sea salt. Bake on the middle rack of a preheated 375-degree-F oven for 8 to 10 minutes. Cool slightly before transferring to a wire rack. *Makes about 5 dozen cookies.*

thumbprint cookies

These little bites can also be made with hazelnuts,
pecans, or macadamia nuts.

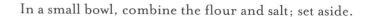

1 cup all-purpose flour

1/4 teaspoon kosher salt

1/2 cup unsalted butter,
softened

1/3 cup superfine sugar

1 teaspoon vanilla extract

1 large egg yolk

3/4 cup finely ground lightly
toasted almonds

Raspberry or strawberry
preserves, or orange
marmalade

Powdered sugar (optional)

In a small bowl, combine the flour and salt; set aside.

In a mixer bowl with the paddle attachment, beat
the butter and sugar until pale yellow and fluffy.
Add the vanilla and egg yolk, beating until well
combined. Mix in the flour mixture and nuts until
the dough is well combined. Form the dough into
1-inch balls and place on a parchment- or Silpat-
lined baking sheet. Make a depression in the center
of each cookie using the handle of a wooden spoon
or your fingertip. Add 1/4 teaspoon preserves or
marmalade in each indentation. Bake for 22 to 25
minutes at 350 degrees F until very lightly browned;
cool slightly. Sprinkle with powdered sugar before
serving, if desired. *Makes 24 cookies.*

triple ginger pecan cookies

Three variations of ginger—fresh, ground, and crystallized—come together
to create a soft, pecan-laced cookie. Just like a ginger cookie should be!

2¼ cups all-purpose flour

1 teaspoon baking soda

2 teaspoons ground
cinnamon

½ teaspoon ground cloves

½ teaspoon ground nutmeg

1 teaspoon ground ginger

1 teaspoon finely grated
fresh ginger

¼ teaspoon kosher salt

1 cup brown sugar,
lightly packed

½ cup unsalted butter,
softened

¼ cup vegetable oil

⅓ cup molasses

1 large egg, room
temperature

½ cup finely chopped
crystallized ginger

1 cup finely chopped pecans

Sugar, for rolling
the cookies

Line two baking sheet pans with parchment paper or
Silpat; set aside.

In a large bowl, sift together the flour, baking soda,
cinnamon, cloves, nutmeg, ground ginger, grated
ginger, and salt; set aside.

In the bowl of an electric mixer, beat the brown
sugar, butter, oil, and molasses on medium speed for
5 minutes. Turn the mixer to low speed, add the egg,
and beat for 1 minute. With the mixer still on low,
slowly add the dry ingredients to the bowl and mix
on medium speed for 2 minutes. Add the crystallized
ginger and pecans and mix until combined.

Use a small 1-inch diameter ice cream scoop or a
teaspoon to form 1-inch balls with the dough and
then roll each in the sugar. Press the dough down
with the bottom of a glass. Place the cookies on the
prepared baking sheet. Bake at 350 degrees F for 10
to 11 minutes. The cookies will be crackled on the top
and soft inside. Let the cookies cool on the baking
sheets for 1 to 2 minutes, then transfer to wire racks
to cool completely. *Makes about 5 dozen cookies.*

walnut and raisin hermits

The perfumed aroma of spices and molasses is so
enticing in these soft, delectable bars.

3/4	cup unsalted butter, softened
1/2	cup sugar
1/2	cup dark brown sugar
2	large eggs
3 1/2	cups all-purpose flour
1/2	teaspoon kosher salt
1	teaspoon baking powder
1	teaspoon ground cinnamon
1	teaspoon ground cloves
1/2	teaspoon ground ginger
1/4	teaspoon ground allspice
1	tablespoon vanilla extract
1/4	cup dark molasses mixed with 1/4 cup warm water
1/2	cup craisins
1/2	cup dark raisins
1	cup coarsely chopped walnuts
1	egg, beaten
	Powdered sugar

In the bowl of a mixer, cream the butter and sugars
until fluffy. Beat in the eggs. Add the flour, salt,
baking powder, cinnamon, cloves, ginger, allspice,
vanilla, and molasses mixture; beat until combined.
Add the craisins, raisins, and walnuts. Beat until just
mixed. Divide the dough into fourths. With floured
hands, form each section into a strip that is 10- x
2 1/2- x 3/4-inch. (I use a ruler to measure and form
the dough into a perfect rectangle.)

Place dough rectangles on two baking sheets lined
with parchment paper. Use enough flour on your
hands to keep dough from sticking. Brush the tops
of each dough strip with the beaten egg. Bake at 350
degrees F for 20 to 22 minutes until cooked through.
Cool for 30 minutes. Using a ruler, cut each strip
into bars 1-inch wide. Sprinkle with powdered sugar.
Makes about 40 bars.

INSTANT COOL
GRATIFICATION

apricot fool

A "fool" is a perfect rich dessert highlighting fresh fruits combined
with whipped cream in layers. Served in a decorative goblet, it can be
assembled hours in advance, and chilled until ready to serve.
This combination of apricots and cream is perfect in midsummer, but the
recipes works with berries as well, especially strawberries all year round.

2 cups halved fresh apricots
(about 8 large apricots)

¼ cup chopped
crystallized ginger

½ cup orange juice

2 tablespoons amaretto
liqueur

1 cup heavy cream

¼ cup powdered sugar

¼ teaspoon almond extract

4 amaretti cookies
for garnish

Combine the apricots, ginger, juice, and liqueur in
a small saucepan. Cover and simmer for 15 minutes
until fruit is soft; cool slightly. Puree in a blender or
food processor and then chill until ready to serve.

In a mixer bowl, beat the cream, sugar, and
almond extract until stiff peaks form. When ready
to assemble, place 2 tablespoons of apricot puree
on bottom of four decorative goblets. Top with 2
tablespoons cream, another 2 tablespoons apricot
puree, and another dollop cream. Serve each with an
amaretti cookie on top. *Serves 4.*

affogato

After a substantial meal, nothing soothes the appetite more than a warm
cup of coffee with a little cream. *Affogato* in Italian means "drowned."
Ice cream is happily submerged in espresso in this recipe. Combined
in a decorative cup, the after-meal delight is easy yet so enjoyable.

1   scoop vanilla gelato
    or ice cream

2   ounces strong hot espresso
    (one shot)

    Grated dark chocolate,
    chocolate-coated
    coffee bean

Place a scoop of gelato or ice cream in a decorative
espresso cup. Slowly pour the hot espresso over the
gelato. Garnish with the grated dark chocolate and/
or a chocolate-coated coffee bean. *This recipe makes one
serving. Line up the espresso cups and repeat to serve affogato to
one, two, or a table of eight.*

almond flan with fresh fruit

Try this classic Spanish dessert with a flair and the addition of almonds and fruit. Remember, this dessert needs to be refrigerated for several hours after baking to allow the custard to chill.

CARAMEL

1½ cups sugar

1 cup sliced almonds

CUSTARD

Zest of 1 orange

2 cups heavy cream

1 cup whole milk

1 teaspoon almond extract

6 large egg yolks

4 large whole eggs

¼ cup honey

Sliced strawberries, blackberries, orange slices, blueberries, or raspberries

Whipped cream

In a heavy saucepan, cook the sugar over medium heat until golden brown. Stir occasionally with a wooden spoon until the sugar is totally melted and medium brown. Don't get discouraged; the sugar crystals will eventually melt and form a light brown caramel. Once the caramel starts to turn a light brown, turn off the heat. The entire process will take about 5 minutes. The sugar will continue to cook after the heat is off. Add the almonds to the caramel. Quickly pour into a 9-inch round ceramic pie pan and tilt pan so that the caramel is an even layer on the bottom; set aside.

In the same saucepan as the sugar was cooked, add the orange zest, cream, milk, and almond extract. Bring to a simmer over medium heat. Turn off the heat; set aside.

In a medium bowl, beat the egg yolks, whole eggs, and honey until frothy. Temper the eggs by whisking half of the hot milk mixture into the eggs, then pour the remaining mixture into the eggs; whisk for 30 seconds. Pour into the caramel-lined pan. Place pie pan in a larger baking pan—large enough so you can add hot tap water to the pan to go halfway up the side of the pie plate. This is called a "bain-marie" or water bath. Cover the pie plate loosely with foil. Bake on the middle rack of a preheated 325-degree-F oven for 1 to 1 ¼ hours, or until a knife inserted in center comes out clean. Allow to cool 1 hour before chilling.

Refrigerate overnight or at least 8 hours. When ready to serve, run a sharp knife around the edge of flan and invert pie pan onto another platter. Cut into 8 wedges and serve with caramel from the pan drizzled on top. Serve with fresh fruit and/or whipped cream. *Serves 8.*

amano chocolate profiteroles with blackberry–pink peppercorn sauce

Profiteroles—cream puff shells stuffed with ice cream—
can be exciting, especially when made with artisan
chocolate and served with a pink peppercorn sauce.

Use a quality dark chocolate for the ultimate in flavor. Amano Artisan
Chocolates, a multi-award winning fine chocolate company
dedicated to small batch manufacturing is located in Orem,
Utah. Their Madagascar dark chocolate has been the recipient
of more than twenty international and American awards.

PROFITEROLE SHELLS

- 1 cup water
- ½ cup unsalted butter, cut into 8 pieces
- 2 ounces grated dark chocolate (I use Amano's Madagascar 70 percent cacao dark chocolate)
- ½ teaspoon kosher salt
- 1 teaspoon sugar
- 1 cup all-purpose flour
- 4 large eggs, room temperature
- 2 pints quality coffee ice cream or gelato (or other chocolate-friendly flavor)

In a medium saucepan, bring the water, butter, chocolate, salt, and sugar to a boil. While the water is boiling, add the flour in one swoop, stirring constantly with a wooden spoon until the dough starts to pull away from the sides of the pan. This entire process takes about 30 seconds. Remove the pan from the heat and transfer the dough to a food processor or the bowl of a mixer. Add eggs to the dough, one at a time, mixing until totally incorporated. (You can also use a wooden spoon and elbow grease to incorporate the eggs one at a time.)

Place a tablespoon of dough on a Silpat- or parchment-lined baking sheet; dough makes about 16 scoops. Dip your finger in water and lightly press any points of dough down to prevent burning. Bake on the middle rack of a preheated 425-degree-F oven

BLACKBERRY-PINK PEPPERCORN SAUCE

- 1 cup Shiraz, Malbec, or any bold red wine
- ½ cup water
- ½ cup sugar
- 1 teaspoon pink peppercorns, crushed lightly
- 2 cups fresh blackberries

for 20 minutes, and then reduce the heat to 350 degrees F for an additional 15 minutes. The shells should be doubled in size and puffed; remove from oven and cool completely.

In a small saucepan, bring the wine, water, sugar, and peppercorns to a simmer; cook for 15 to 20 minutes until the sugar syrup reduces by half. Remove the peppercorns (or leave them in the syrup if you want a strong peppery flavor). Add the blackberries to the syrup. Cook on low for 5 minutes just until warmed through and thickened slightly.

Cut the chocolate shells in half horizontally. Fill each with a scoop of ice cream. (This step can be done ahead, and the profiteroles frozen until ready to serve.) Place a profiterole on a serving dish, drizzle with some of the warmed blackberry sauce, and serve at once. *Makes about 16 profiteroles.*

bananas foster

This is my go-to dessert for all seasons, as I almost always have bananas, an orange, and vanilla ice cream in the house. The other ingredients—butter, cinnamon, dark rum, orange liqueur, and brown sugar—are staples in the cupboard. It's a 5-minute assembly, and wonderful entertainment for your guests.

4 tablespoons unsalted butter

1/2 teaspoon ground cinnamon

1 cup brown sugar

Juice and zest of 1 large orange

3 firm bananas, peeled and cut into 1/2-inch-thick slices on the diagonal

1/2 cup dark rum

1/4 cup triple sec or other orange-flavored liqueur

6 scoops good-quality vanilla or butter pecan ice cream

Thin strips of orange zest

In a medium skillet, heat the butter until melted. Add the cinnamon, brown sugar, and orange juice and zest; cook on medium heat until sugar is melted. Take the pan off the heat to prevent a flair up of the alcohol and add the sliced bananas, rum, and liqueur. Return pan to heat and cook over low until bananas are heated through, about 1 minute. Place a scoop of ice cream in a serving bowl and top with bananas and rum sauce. Garnish with orange zest. *Serves 6.*

chocolate amaretto mousse

The heavenly combination of chocolate and almonds are
whipped together to create this ethereal dessert. It needs at least
6 hours of chilling before serving, so prepare ahead.

1 pound semisweet
   chocolate chips

2 large whole eggs

4 large egg yolks

4 large egg whites

2 cups very cold
   heavy cream

1/3 cup powdered sugar

2 tablespoons amaretto
   liqueur or 1 teaspoon
   almond extract

TOPPING

1/2 cup heavy cream

2 tablespoons
   powdered sugar

1 tablespoon amaretto
   liqueur or 1/4 teaspoon
   almond extract

Shaved chocolate

In the top of a double boiler over simmering water
(or place a metal bowl over a saucepan of simmering
water), melt the chocolate, stirring often with a
wooden spoon. Remove the bowl of melted chocolate
from the heat; cool for 5 minutes. Whisk in the whole
eggs and the egg yolks, one at a time. Do this quickly
so that the eggs do not overcook in the chocolate.
Transfer to a large bowl.

In a mixer bowl, beat the egg whites until stiff peaks
form; set aside in another bowl.

In the same mixer bowl you used to beat the egg
whites, beat the heavy cream, sugar, and amaretto
or almond extract until stiff peaks form. Fold the
cream into the melted chocolate mixture. Fold the
beaten egg whites into the chocolate mixture. Do
not overmix. Transfer the mousse into goblets or
decorative cups. Chill at least 6 hours or overnight to
allow the mousse to set up.

When ready to serve, beat heavy cream for topping
with sugar for 1 minute until thickened slightly. Add
the amaretto or almond extract and beat until stiff
peaks form, about 2 minutes on medium speed. Put
a dollop of cream on each portion of the mousse and
garnish with shaved chocolate. *Serves 8.*

chilled cantaloupe-mango soup

The welcoming hue of pale orange in this cool cantaloupe-
and mango-infused soup with honey makes for an easy
summer intermezzo or a sweet first course.

2 cups diced cantaloupe

1 cup diced fresh mango

1/2 cup honey

1/2 cup white wine or
champagne (or
white grape juice)

1/2 cup orange juice

1/2 teaspoon kosher salt

6 ounces plain Greek yogurt

1/8 teaspoon ground nutmeg

Yogurt

Place the cantaloupe, mango, honey, wine or grape juice, orange juice, salt, yogurt, and nutmeg in a food processor or blender; puree until smooth, about 1 to 2 minutes. Pour into bowls and chill for at least 1 hour before serving. Garnish with a dollop of yogurt. *Makes about 1 quart soup.*

creamy limoncello shooters

Are you searching for that one perfect sweet alcoholic-infused ending to a meal? Try Limoncello, cream, and a sprinkle of lime zest for the ultimate sweet finale. This recipe makes one shooter, but you can line up the glasses and make as many as desired.

2   tablespoons chilled Limoncello (Italian lemon liqueur)

2   tablespoons heavy cream

1/4 teaspoon grated lime zest

Place the Limoncello in a chilled shooter glass. Top with cream and the lime zest. *Serves 1.*

cool cucumber mint sorbet

Cucumbers, mint, and lime juice are frozen in a perfect
concoction to create a sorbet for the ultimate "coolness."
Lovely to eat on a hot summer evening.

3 cups diced cucumber
    (about 3 medium peeled
    and seeded cucumbers)

1/4 cup chopped fresh
     spearmint or
     peppermint leaves

1/2 cup fresh lime juice

1 tablespoon corn syrup

3/4 cup sugar

3/4 cup cold water

1/4 cup Limoncello (Italian
     lemon liqueur)

12 mint sprigs

12 lime slices

In a food processor, puree the cucumber, mint, and
lime juice. Add the corn syrup; set aside.

In a 2-quart saucepan, bring the sugar and water to
a boil, then reduce to medium heat and cook until
sugar is dissolved, about 3 minutes, to make a simple
syrup. The mixture should measure 1 1/4 cups; cool
slightly. Add the cucumber mixture to the simple
syrup. Chill for at least 2 hours and up to 8 hours.

Pour into an ice cream maker and follow the
manufacturer's directions for completing the sorbet
process. The sorbet will have a slushy texture; if a
firmer consistency is desired, transfer the sorbet
to a plastic container and freeze for an additional
2 hours. Scoop a 1/2-cup serving of sorbet into a
small serving bowl, top with 1 teaspoon Limoncello,
and serve at once with a mint sprig and lime slice.
Makes 12 servings.

fig, almond, and honey ice cream

When fresh figs are in season during the summer and early autumn
months, combine the sweetness of figs with honey and almond
for the ideal ice cream combination. Served with biscotti and
a cup of espresso, this dessert is an aromatic Italian delight.

1   cup cold whole milk

1   cup sugar

3   cups cold heavy cream

1   teaspoon vanilla extract

1   teaspoon almond extract

1   cup finely chopped
    fresh black mission
    or brown turkey figs,
    stems removed

3/4   cup finely chopped
    almonds

1/4   cup honey

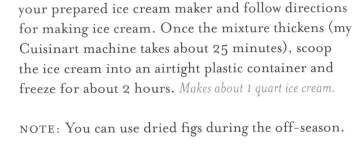

In a mixing bowl, beat the milk and sugar for
2 minutes on medium speed until sugar is dissolved
and mixture starts to froth. Stir in the heavy cream,
vanilla, and almond extract. Beat in the figs,
almonds, and honey until combined, about 20
seconds. Do not overbeat. Transfer the mixture into
your prepared ice cream maker and follow directions
for making ice cream. Once the mixture thickens (my
Cuisinart machine takes about 25 minutes), scoop
the ice cream into an airtight plastic container and
freeze for about 2 hours. *Makes about 1 quart ice cream.*

NOTE: You can use dried figs during the off-season.

egg cream float

For New York City-ites, an egg cream is a local favorite beverage. Egg creams became so popular that author Elliot Willensky wrote in his book *When Brooklyn Was the World,* "A candy store minus an egg cream, in Brooklyn at least, was as difficult to conceive of as the Earth without gravity."

Containing neither eggs nor cream, for me an egg cream conjures up memories of sitting up at a soda fountain, watching the seltzer foaming in a glass, sipping this classic cold beverage through a straw, and reveling in the flavors of chocolate, milk, and seltzer. Add a scoop of ice cream and it's a float for a more substantial drink.

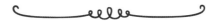

2 tablespoons U-bet Chocolate Syrup or other chocolate syrup

½ cup whole milk (no substitutes)

Cold seltzer or club soda

Scoop of chocolate ice cream

Place the chocolate syrup in a tall 12-ounce soda glass. Add the milk; stir once. Add enough seltzer or club soda to come within 1-inch of the top of the glass. Float the scoop of ice cream on top; serve with a straw. *Makes 1 serving.*

NOTE: U-bet Chocolate Syrup is the brand of choice for this drink. Manufactured in Brooklyn, it can be ordered online or found in specialty food shops around the country.

lavender-thyme infused panna cotta with island berry compote

Creamy panna cotta ("cooked cream" in Italian) heady with summer lavender and fresh thyme and topped with berries is everything one dreams of in a sweet finale!

1 tablespoon lavender buds

1 tablespoon fresh
   thyme leaves

2 cups heavy cream

1/2 cup sugar

1 envelope unflavored
   Knox gelatin

1/2 cup half-and-half

2 cups sour cream

ISLAND BERRY COMPOTE

4 cups mixed berries
   (raspberries, blueberries,
   blackberries, loganberries,
   strawberries, and
   marionberries)

1/2 cup sugar

1 teaspoon cornstarch

2 tablespoons lavender
   honey (optional)

   Lavender buds, mint
   leaf, thyme sprig

Place the lavender and thyme leaves in a saucepan with cream and sugar. Bring to a low simmer and cook for 3 to 4 minutes, stirring to dissolve the sugar. Remove from heat; allow the herbs to steep in the cream for 5 to 10 minutes, depending on the intensity desired. While the cream is steeping, soften the gelatin in the half-and-half in a small bowl. Strain the cream through a sieve and place back in the saucepan. Bring heat back to low. Cream should not be brought to a simmer, just warmed through.

Add the gelatin mixture and whisk to incorporate. Remove from heat and whisk in the sour cream. Taste for seasoning. The gelatin should be incorporated and the sour cream smooth. Pour the panna cotta cream into individual serving glasses, molds, or ramekins. Chill in refrigerator for at least 4 hours or until set firm. (This can be made a day ahead.)

In a saucepan, bring the berries, sugar, cornstarch, and honey if using to a simmer over low heat, stirring often. Sauce should be thickened slightly, but not cloudy. Remove from heat and cool. Serve a small serving on top of the panna cotta and garnish with lavender buds, mint leaf, or thyme. *Serves 8.*

ginger thins ice cream sandwiches with caramel pear slices

A delightful dessert for little kids—both those small in stature as well as those young at heart. Make ahead, put in freezer, and serve with caramel pear slices or just as is. In the fall months, the spiced flavors of the season work beautifully together in this quick dessert.

ICE CREAM SANDWICHES

24 ginger thin cookies (such as Anna's thin cookies)

1 quart pumpkin or apple pie ice cream (seasonally available), or use cinnamon, butter pecan, or any exotic flavor

1 cup finely chopped nuts (hazelnuts, pecans, walnuts, or almonds)

CARAMEL PEAR SLICES

4 tablespoons unsalted butter

2 D'Anjou or Bartlett pears, peeled, cored, and thinly sliced

¼ cup brown sugar

1 teaspoon pumpkin pie spice

½ cup heavy cream

Place 12 ginger thins on a work surface, bottom side of cookie facing up. Using a small ice cream scoop, place a portion of ice cream on each cookie, then top with another ginger thin. Place the chopped nuts in a shallow dish. Roll the sides of the ice cream sandwiches in the nuts so they are lightly coated. Place on a baking sheet and freeze until ready to serve.

In a medium skillet, heat the butter until melted. Add the pears and cook for 2 minutes, stirring often. Add the brown sugar, pumpkin pie spice, and cream; cook on low for 5 minutes. Mixture should be syrupy at this point. Chill until ready to serve.

Place 2 to 3 pear slices on bottom of serving dish. Top with one or two ice cream sandwiches. Drizzle with some of the reserved caramel-pear sauce and serve at once. *Serves 6 to 12.*

nutella malt with a kick

An adult version of a chocolate malt with the addition of Godiva
chocolate liqueur creates a liquid dessert to savor alongside a burger,
after a meal, or just because it's a sweltering Saturday afternoon.

1   tablespoon Nutella

1   large scoop chocolate
     ice cream

1   cup whole milk

1   tablespoon powdered malt

2   tablespoons Godiva
     chocolate liqueur

2   to 3 tablespoons
     whipped cream

1   Baci (Italian chocolate-
     hazelnut candy),
     finely chopped (about
     1 tablespoon)

In a blender, add the Nutella, ice cream, milk, malt,
and liqueur. Power on high for 10 to 20 seconds
until smooth. Pour into four 3-ounce glasses. Top
with whipped cream and Baci candy. Serve each with
a straw! *Makes 4 tasting-size servings.*

minty strawberry-
nectarine gelato

A hint of mint and a creamy fruity combination of strawberries
and succulent nectarines create a dessert for all ages. There are
many steps to this recipe. Read the recipe first, and then continue.
Don't be discouraged. The final results will be your reward.

1	pint fresh strawberries, hulled and chopped
2	large nectarines, peeled, pitted, and chopped
1	cup sugar
1¼	cups half-and-half
½	cup fresh spearmint or peppermint leaves, coarsely chopped
6	large egg yolks
½	cup fat-free powdered milk
1	cup heavy cream
1	cup half-and-half
2	teaspoons vanilla extract

Place the fruit in a food processor and puree until
smooth. Set aside. In a heavy-duty 2-quart saucepan,
combine the sugar, 1 ¼ cups half-and-half, and mint
leaves. Over medium heat, whisk the mixture until the
sugar dissolves, about 2 minutes. Allow the mint leaves
to steep for 5 minutes. Strain through a sieve and
discard the mint. Return the mixture to the saucepan.

In a medium bowl, beat the egg yolks until thickened,
about 2 minutes. Add ½ cup of the warmed half-
and-half mixture to the eggs and continue to beat
another minute. Add the entire egg mixture to
the saucepan along with remaining half-and-half
mixture. Over medium heat, whisk constantly for 5
to 8 minutes until thickened to a custard consistency
and mixture registers 180 degrees F on an instant-
read thermometer. Whisk in the powdered milk,
heavy cream, 1 cup half-and-half, and vanilla. Pour
the entire combination through a strainer into a large
bowl. Stir in the reserved fruit puree. Refrigerate
for 6 hours. Follow the directions on your ice cream
maker for making gelato. Freeze the gelato until
desired consistency. *Makes about 1 quart gelato.*

lemon crème atop fruit-stuffed crêpes

Crêpes can be such an underappreciated dessert. But when stuffed and topped properly, crêpes are the showcase of the meal. This recipe can be done in stages. Crêpes and crème made a day ahead and the filling the day of. Then all that remains is the assembly process. Voila! French flair for brunch, dessert, or just because.

CRÊPE BATTER

- 2 large eggs, room temperature
- 3/4 cup whole milk
- 1/2 cup water
- 1 cup all-purpose flour
- 3 tablespoons unsalted butter, melted
- 1 teaspoon sugar
- 1/2 teaspoon kosher salt

SUMMER FRUIT FILLING

- 2 cups mixed fresh berries (raspberries, blueberries, blackberries, or sliced strawberries)
- 1 cup thinly sliced peaches
- 1 cup thinly sliced plums or apricots
- 1 tablespoon sugar
- 1 tablespoon orange-flavored liqueur

In a blender or food processor, blend all crêpe batter ingredients for 30 seconds or until smooth. Refrigerate the batter for at least 1 hour and up to 24 hours.

Heat a nonstick 7- or 8-inch crêpe pan over medium-high heat and add 1/2 teaspoon unsalted butter to pan when hot, then wipe out with a paper towel. Pour 2 tablespoons of the batter into the center of the pan and swirl to spread. Cook for 30 seconds, flip, and cook another 10 seconds. Remove to a plate and continue until all the batter is used. (You can also use an electric crêpe pan—just follow manufacturer's directions.)

For the summer filling, combine all the ingredients in a bowl; allow to macerate for at least 30 minutes and up to 2 hours.

For the fall filling, in a small saucepan, heat the butter and sauté the apples and pears for 2 minutes, stirring often. Add the brown sugar, raisins,

FALL FRUIT FILLING

- 2 tablespoons butter
- 2 crisp baking apples, such as Granny Smith, or honeycrisp, peeled, cored, and finely diced
- 2 Bartlett pears, peeled, cored, and finely diced
- 1 tablespoon brown sugar
- ¼ cup golden raisins
- ¼ cup dried cranberries
   Juice of 1 orange
- 1 teaspoon pumpkin pie spice

LEMON CRÈME

- 8 ounces good-quality bottled lemon curd
- 8 ounces crème fraîche
   Zest and juice of 1 lemon

cranberries, orange juice, and pumpkin pie spice. Cover; simmer for 5 minutes. Cool, then refrigerate until ready to use.

For the crème, combine all the ingredients in a bowl; whisk well and chill until ready to serve.

TO ASSEMBLE: Place a warmed crêpe on a work surface and place 2 tablespoons filling of choice in center of crêpe. Fold into fourths and top with Lemon Crème. *Serve 2 per person.*

grilled peaches with mascarpone on grilled pound cake

Grilling fruit brings out the sweetness. Grilling pound cake also brings out the sweetness and buttery flavor of the cake. Combine the two with a creamy mascarpone topping, and it's summer on a plate, assembled in just minutes.

4   yellow or white firm peaches, cut in half, pits removed

Canola oil

8   (1-inch-thick) slices pound cake

MASCARPONE CREAM

8   ounces mascarpone cheese

2   tablespoons half-and-half

Zest and juice of 1 orange

1/2   teaspoon almond extract

1/4   cup powdered sugar

Brush both sides of the peach halves with oil. Grill over medium-low heat for 3 minutes per side until grill marks appear and peaches soften slightly.

Mix the ingredients for the cream with a whisk. (This can be made ahead and chilled.)

Grill slices of pound cake over medium-low heat for 3 minutes per side. Place a slice of pound cake on each plate. Top each slice with one peach half, cut into quarters, and drizzle with the cream. *Serves 8.*

red, white, and blue ice cream sundaes with caramel pecan sauce

Patriotic colors of red, white, and blue top this easy sundae drizzled with caramel pecan sauce.

FRUIT COMPOTE

- 4 cups sliced strawberries and/or raspberries
- 2 white peaches, pitted and cut into 1-inch dice
- 2 cups fresh blueberries
- 1/4 cup sugar
- 2 tablespoons dark rum or orange juice

CARAMEL PECAN SAUCE

- 2 cups bottled good-quality caramel sauce
- 1 cup chopped toasted pecans
- 1 teaspoon ground cinnamon

ICE CREAM

- 1 quart good-quality vanilla ice cream

Combine all ingredients for fruit compote in a bowl; refrigerate until ready to serve.

Place the caramel sauce, pecans, and cinnamon in a small saucepan and heat until just warmed through.

Place a scoop of ice cream in a serving bowl, top with some of the sauce, and top with the fresh compote. *Serves 8.*

prosecco zabaglione with fresh strawberries

Prosecco is an Italian sparkling wine that pairs perfectly with *zabaglione*, the Italian version of the French *sabayon*. It is lighter in taste than the traditional composition which has Marsala wine. This dessert takes a few minutes to literally whip together and makes for a good show for guests.

8 large egg yolks, room temperature

½ cup sugar

1 cup Italian Prosecco (or French champagne, California white wine, or Spanish cava)

1 quart fresh strawberries, hulled and quartered

¼ cup sugar

Mint leaves

Lemon peel twists

Place the egg yolks and sugar in a 6-quart stainless steel mixing bowl. Beat with a hand mixer for 1 minute until frothy. In a saucepan that will hold the mixing bowl securely on top without the bottom of the bowl touching the water, bring water to a boil, then reduce heat to a simmer. If the bowl touches the water, the eggs will cook too quickly and be "scrambled" on the bottom. Beat the egg and sugar mixture with the hand mixer over the pan of just simmering water until it doubles in volume. Slowly pour in the Prosecco, beating constantly. Continue to beat until the mixture triples in volume. This entire process takes about 8 minutes. The zabaglione should be thick and very light yellow in color at this point. Remove from heat.

Combine the quartered strawberries and ¼ cup sugar in a bowl. Mix well. Place the strawberries into decorative glasses or bowls. Top with dollops of the zabaglione. Garnish with mint leaves and lemon peel twists and serve at once. *Serves 8.*

sweet corn crème brûlée
with blueberries

Corn and blueberries you say? A strange combination,
but they work in this unusual crème brûlée.

CUSTARD

- 2 cups fresh corn kernels, scraped from 2 ears of corn
- 4 tablespoons unsalted butter
- 3 1/2 cups half-and-half
- 1/8 teaspoon ground nutmeg
- 1 teaspoon vanilla extract
- 8 large egg yolks
- 3/4 cup sugar

TOPPING

- 1 cup fresh blueberries
- 1/4 cup sugar

Place the corn in a saucepan with the butter; cook for 3 to 5 minutes until corn is softened and fragrant; set aside. Heat the half-and-half, nutmeg, and vanilla in a saucepan until cream is bubbling slightly. Add the cooked corn to the half-and-half mixture and let steep for 15 to 20 minutes. Place the mixture in a blender or food processor and blend until corn is slightly pureed, but not completely liquified.

Beat the egg yolks and 3/4 cup sugar in a mixer until light yellow and thickened. Slowly add the corn mixture to the egg yolks, beating until completely mixed. Pour into eight 1-cup ramekins, filling each almost full. Place the ramekins in a baking pan. Pour hot water into the baking pan until it is halfway up the sides of the ramekins. Bake on the middle rack of the oven at 300 degrees F for 35 to 40 minutes until set. Cool in refrigerator for 2 to 24 hours, covered lightly with plastic wrap.

When ready to serve, lightly sprinkle the tops of the custard with the remaining sugar. Heat a broiler and brown the tops of the custard for 3 to 4 minutes just until sugar melts and is golden. Top each with 2 tablespoons blueberries while the sugar is still warm. Chill again for a few hours until sugar hardens. *Makes 8 servings.*

strawberry panna cotta with strawberry-basil balsamic compote

At the peak of strawberry season, basil is also making its summer appearance. Combining the two in a compote topping for a delicate strawberry-scented panna cotta makes for a July culinary memory.

2 cups heavy cream

¹/₂ cup sugar

1 cup sour cream

1 teaspoon vanilla extract

¹/₂ cup half-and-half

1 envelope unflavored Knox gelatin

1 pint fresh strawberries, hulled and cut into quarters

¹/₄ cup sugar

STRAWBERRY-BASIL BALSAMIC COMPOTE

2 cups diced fresh strawberries

¹/₄ cup sugar

2 tablespoons chopped fresh basil

2 tablespoons balsamic vinegar

8 ounces sour cream or crème fraîche

In a medium saucepan, heat the cream with ¹/₂ cup sugar for 2 to 3 minutes until warmed through and the sugar has dissolved. Stir in the sour cream and vanilla.

In a smaller saucepan, heat the half-and-half with the gelatin until the gelatin is dissolved and is mixed into the half-and-half. Add this to the warmed cream mixture and whisk completely until combined.

Place strawberries and ¹/₄ cup sugar in a food processor or blender and pulse on and off until finely chopped. Transfer to the cream mixture. Pour evenly into martini glasses or goblets or use decorative 6-ounce molds that have been sprayed with nonstick cooking spray. Chill for at least 4 hours until the panna cotta has set. Turn out the molded panna cotta onto serving dishes.

In a small saucepan, simmer the berries and ¹/₄ cup sugar for 2 to 3 minutes just until the berries have warmed through and sugar has dissolved. Stir in the basil and balsamic; remove from heat and chill until ready to serve. Top panna cottas with a tablespoon of compote and a dollop of sour cream or crème fraîche just before serving. *Serves 8.*

zesty lemon mousse
with blueberries

Citrus zest—whether lemon, lime, orange, tangelo, or whatever is in season—combined with fresh fruit creates a magical combination. And when both lemon and blueberries are in a creamy and tangy mousse, it couldn't be a better ending to a meal. Be forewarned: this entire process dirties five bowls, but don't get discouraged. It's worth it.

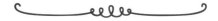

3/4 cup freshly squeezed lemon juice

Zest of 1 large lemon (about 1 tablespoon)

6 large egg yolks, room temperature

2 large whole eggs, room temperature

1 cup sugar

1 envelope unflavored Knox gelatin

3 tablespoons cold water

6 large egg whites, room temperature

1 1/2 cups heavy whipping cream

2 cups fresh blueberries

2 tablespoons sugar

In a medium stainless steel mixing bowl or in a double-boiler pot, beat the lemon juice, lemon zest, egg yolks, whole eggs, and 1 cup sugar until well combined. Place the bowl over a pot of simmering water, making sure the bottom of the bowl does not touch the water. Whisk the mixture for 5 to 8 minutes constantly until thickened to the consistency of pudding. (This mixture is called "lemon curd.") Remove the bowl from the heat.

In a small bowl, dissolve the gelatin in the cold water for 2 to 3 minutes until the gelatin is softened. Whisk the gelatin into the hot lemon curd. Set aside until cooled to room temperature, whisking occasionally.

In a bowl, beat the egg whites until stiff. In another bowl, beat the cream until stiff peaks form.

Mix the blueberries and the sugar in another bowl.

(continued)

zesty lemon mousse with blueberries (cont.)

8 lemon strips

8 mint sprigs

Fold the whipped cream into the cooled lemon mixture. Then fold the whipped egg whites into the cooled lemon mixture. Do not overmix, but make sure the gelatin mixture is incorporated into the cream and egg whites. Divide the lemon mixture among goblets or serving dishes. Top each with blueberries. Add the remaining lemon mousse and blueberries. Refrigerate for at least 3 hours before serving to allow the gelatin to set up. (I usually make this dessert early in the morning or a day before serving.) Garnish with fresh lemon strips and an additional dollop of whipped cream, if desired. *Serves 8.*

MORNING GLORIES

apple turnovers

Quick to prepare, deliciously warm and comforting, turnovers made with puff pastry and filled with spiced apples are a sweet treat for breakfast, a snack, or a take-along picnic.

4   tablespoons butter

4   Granny Smith apples, peeled, cored, and chopped

½   cup raisins

¼   cup sugar

¼   cup brown sugar

Juice of 1 lemon

1   tablespoon all-purpose flour

½   teaspoon cinnamon

¼   teaspoon nutmeg

¼   teaspoon kosher salt

1   package (17.3 ounces) puff pastry, thawed

1   egg beaten with 1 tablespoon cream (egg wash)

2   tablespoons turbinado (raw sugar)

In a large skillet, heat the butter and sauté the apples and raisins until apples are soft. Add the sugars, lemon juice, flour, cinnamon, nutmeg, and salt. Cook another 5 minutes; cool slightly.

Place the two sheets of puff pastry on a work surface and cut each into eighths. Place about 1 tablespoon filling in the center of each; fold over into a triangle. Crimp edges. Place the turnovers on a parchment- or Silpat-lined baking sheet. Brush each with the egg wash and sprinkle with turbinado. Bake on the middle rack of a preheated 400-degree-F oven for 20 to 22 minutes until puffed and golden brown. *Makes 16 mini turnovers.*

aebleskivers

Shaped like doughnut holes, these Danish morsels of goodness are for breakfast, a snack, or a late-night treat. The only requirement is an aebleskiver pan—a cast-iron pan with seven indentations for the batter to cook and turn so it can brown easily on all sides. Somehow, they come out looking like perfect spheres. There are as many recipes for aebleskivers as there are Danes. So, if your grandmother's is better, go for it.

Special equipment:
aebleskiver pan
(available in all gourmet shops and cookstores)

2 cups all-purpose flour

1 teaspoon baking powder

1 teaspoon baking soda

1/2 teaspoon ground cardamom

1/2 teaspoon kosher salt

1/2 cup sugar

3 large egg yolks

1 teaspoon vanilla extract

2 cups buttermilk

3 large egg whites

1 tablespoon unsalted butter

Raspberry or strawberry preserves

Powdered sugar

In a medium bowl, combine the flour, baking powder, baking soda, cardamom, salt, and sugar.

In another bowl, beat the egg yolks, vanilla, and buttermilk with a whisk or handheld mixer until frothy. Stir the dry ingredients into the wet ingredients just to combine.

In another bowl, beat the egg whites until frothy and stiff peaks form. Gently fold the egg whites into the batter.

Rub a little of the unsalted butter into each indentation of a well-heated aebleskiver pan. With a paper towel, remove excess butter. Place about 1 tablespoon batter in each indentation, top with about 1/2 teaspoon of preserves of choice, and add another tablespoon of batter on top. Cook until the sides are set and bottom is golden brown, about 2 minutes. Using two wooden skewers, carefully turn the aebleskivers over to cook the other side. Cook for 1 to 2 minutes more. Transfer to a platter, dust with powdered sugar, and serve hot. Repeat with remaining batter. *Makes about 3 dozen.*

banana granola muffins

Bananas, granola, and a garnish of a blackberry in one
delectable muffin is the ideal morning pick-me-up.

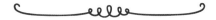

6 tablespoons unsalted
   butter, softened

1/2 cup sugar

2 large eggs

2 large ripe bananas,
   smashed

1 1/2 cups all-purpose flour

1/2 cup granola

1/2 teaspoon kosher salt

2 teaspoons baking powder

1/4 teaspoon baking soda

1/2 cup granola

12 large blackberries

In a bowl, cream the butter and sugar until light
yellow and fluffy, about 2 minutes on medium speed.
Add the eggs and beat another minute. Add the
bananas and beat for another 30 seconds.

In a bowl, combine the dry ingredients of flour,
1/2 cup granola, salt, baking powder, and baking soda.
Add the dry ingredients to the butter mixture and
beat just until combined. Do not overmix.

Spray a 12-cup muffin tin with vegetable oil or
nonstick cooking spray. Fill each muffin cup three-
fourths full with batter. Sprinkle evenly with the
remaining 1/2 cup granola and press a blackberry
into batter in each cup. Bake on the middle rack of a
preheated 350-degree-F oven for 20 to 25 minutes
until golden brown. *Makes 12 muffins.*

lemon–black currant oatmeal muffins

Fresh black currants, when available in summer, are
delicious and quite unique. When currants are out of season,
substitute fresh blueberries for a burst of flavor.

TOPPING

¹/₂	cup quick-cooking oats
2	tablespoons firmly packed brown sugar
¹/₄	teaspoon pumpkin pie spice
1	tablespoon dried currants

MUFFIN MIXTURE

1	cup all-purpose flour
1¹/₄	cups quick-cooking oats
¹/₂	cup sugar
1	tablespoon baking powder
¹/₄	teaspoon kosher salt
¹/₂	teaspoon pumpkin pie spice
1	cup whole milk
1	large egg
1	tablespoon canola oil
2	teaspoons grated lemon zest
1	teaspoon vanilla extract
1	cup fresh black currants or blueberries

In a small bowl, combine the oats, brown sugar, pumpkin pie spice, and dried currants; set aside.

In a medium bowl, mix the flour, oats, sugar, baking powder, salt, and pumpkin pie spice.

In another bowl, whisk the milk, egg, oil, lemon zest, and vanilla until blended. Pour egg mixture into the dry ingredients and mix just until blended. Fold the currants or berries into the batter. Do not overmix. Divide the mixture among 12 paper-lined muffin cups. Sprinkle with the oatmeal topping. Bake on the middle rack of a 400-degree-F oven for 18 to 20 minutes until muffins are cooked through (test with a wooden skewer). Cool slightly and serve. *Makes 12.*

fruit and cheese almond danish

These Danish are just as scrumptious as those from the local
bakery, but are served warm from the oven. Cream cheese, lemon
zest, and fruit all encompassed in a pastry. Delectable!

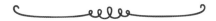

1   package (17.3 ounces)
    frozen puff pastry,
    thawed

8   ounces cream cheese,
    softened

1   large egg

1/4 cup powdered sugar

1   teaspoon lemon zest

1/2 teaspoon vanilla extract

1   cup fresh berries
    (blackberries,
    blueberries, raspberries,
    or sliced strawberries)

1/2 cup sliced almonds

    Powdered sugar

Place the pastry sheets on a work surface and cut each
sheet into fourths. Have two baking sheets lined with
Silpat or parchment paper.

In a medium bowl, whisk the cream cheese, egg,
powdered sugar, lemon zest, and vanilla until
smooth. Divide the mixture among the eight squares
of pastry, placing about 2 tablespoons in the center of
each pastry. Top each with 3 to 4 berries.

Cut a 1-inch slit in the corner of each pastry, then
fold the pastry over the cheese so that just the center
is exposed. Sprinkle with sliced almonds. Place each
Danish square on the prepared baking sheets. Bake
on the middle rack of a preheated 425-degree-F oven
for 20 minutes until the pastry is golden brown and
crispy. Remove from oven, cool slightly, and sprinkle
with powdered sugar before serving. *Makes 8.*

lemon blueberry scones

I usually make these scones with half-and-half. They are
more firm and crumbly, like an English breakfast scone. Buttermilk
makes a lighter scone, and of course, has fewer calories.

SCONES

- 2 cups all-purpose flour
- 2 cups cake flour
- 1/2 cup sugar
- 1 heaping tablespoon
  baking powder
- 1/2 teaspoon baking soda
- 1/2 teaspoon kosher salt
- 1 cup cold unsalted butter,
  cut into small pieces
- 1 cup fresh blueberries
- 2 teaspoons finely
  grated lemon zest
- About 1 cup half-and-
  half or buttermilk
- Sanding sugar (optional)

In a medium bowl, combine the flours, sugar, baking powder, baking soda, and salt; mix. Add the butter and with a pastry cutter, cut in until the size of peas. Add the blueberries and lemon zest; mix. With a wooden spoon or heavy-duty spatula, mix in enough half-and-half or buttermilk to make the batter just moist, not too wet. The dough should hold together when formed into a small ball.

Feel free to use an ice cream scoop or biscuit cutter to form the scones. If using an ice cream scoop, place 15 scoops of dough on each of the two Silpat- or parchment-lined baking sheets.

If using a biscuit cutter, divide the dough in half. Spread some flour on a work surface and press each half of the dough into a circle about 10 x 3/4 inch thick, using more flour on top of the circle as needed. With a 2-inch biscuit cutter, cut out 15 scones per circle of dough. Place on the baking sheets. Form any leftover dough into more scones.

Sprinkle with sanding sugar or bake and then glaze after the scones have slightly cooled. Bake on the middle rack of a 375-degree-F oven (one sheet at a

(continued)

lemon blueberry scones (cont.)

GLAZE

1/3 cup fresh lemon juice

2 1/2 cups powdered sugar

time) for 20 minutes. Remove from oven and cool slightly if using the glaze.

In a bowl, whisk the lemon juice and powdered sugar until smooth. With a fork, drizzle the glaze back and forth over the scones. *Makes 30 small scones.*

VARIATIONS

Cinnamon, Brown Sugar, and Golden Raisin Scones: In a small skillet, heat 2 tablespoons unsalted butter. Add 1/2 cup brown sugar, 1 teaspoon ground cinnamon, and 1 cup golden raisins. Mix over low heat until the sugar has softened, about 1 minute. Cool for 10 minutes. Fold the mixture into the batter after the half-and-half has been added. Do not overmix. Form the scones and bake as directed.

Currant, Pecan, and Lemon Scones: Stir 1 cup currants, 2 teaspoons lemon zest, and 1/2 cup finely chopped toasted pecans into the dry ingredients before the half-and-half is added. Do not overmix. Form the scones and bake as directed.

Mixed Berry Orange Scones: Use 1 1/2 cups mixed berries (blueberries, raspberries, blackberries), thawed if frozen, and 2 teaspoons finely grated orange zest. Fold the berries and orange zest into the dry ingredients before the half-and-half is added. Do not overmix. Form the scones and bake as directed.

very marion-bear-y claws

Warm from the oven, bear claws filled with preserves and cream cheese are the ideal breakfast treat. Allow several hours of preparation time from the rising of the dough to the baking process. The sweet dough can be used in other applications as well. See the variations listed at the end of the recipe.

SWEET DOUGH

1	package active dry yeast
¼	cup warm water (110°F)
1	cup whole milk
¼	cup sugar
4	tablespoons unsalted butter
1	egg, room temperature
½	teaspoon kosher salt
3½	cups all-purpose flour
1	cup marionberry, blackberry, raspberry, strawberry, or loganberry preserves or jam
4	ounces cream cheese, cut into 16 pieces

Place yeast in a small bowl and pour warm water over the top. Cover and let stand in a warm place. Heat milk to scalding and then add the sugar and butter; transfer to a medium bowl and cool to lukewarm, about 20 minutes.

Beat the yeast mixture, egg, and salt into cooled milk mixture. Add 2 cups flour and beat well. Gradually add remaining flour to form a soft dough. Place in a clean, lightly greased bowl and turn once to grease both sides. Cover and let stand in a warm place until the dough has risen to double, about 2 hours.

Separate dough into two balls. Sprinkle a generous amount of flour onto a work surface. Using one dough ball at a time, roll dough into a rectangle about 12 x 10 inches. Slice dough rectangle lengthwise down the middle and then slice each half into 4 strips to form 8 rectangles total. Spoon a teaspoon of jam and place 1 piece of cream cheese in the center of each rectangle. Fold the dough over the filling and secure edges to seal by crimping with a fork. Cut three distinct slits about 1 inch long on the folded side of the bear's paw. These create the claws and allow the filling to vent. Repeat for second ball of dough.

(continued)

very marion-bear-y claws (cont.)

ICING

- 1 cup powdered sugar
- 1 tablespoon whole milk

Place 8 bear claws on a baking sheet lined with Silpat or parchment paper. Repeat with remaining bear claws on a second baking sheet. Place on the middle rack of a preheated 375-degree-F oven and bake, one sheet at time, for 20 minutes or until golden brown. When the bear claws are out of the oven, mix powdered sugar and milk together and drizzle over the warm rolls to ice. *Makes 16 pastries.*

VARIATIONS USING THE SWEET DOUGH

Orange Rolls

- 1 recipe Sweet Dough (see page 91)
- 1/2 cup unsalted butter, softened
- Finely grated zest of 2 large oranges
- 1/2 cup sugar

Roll out each ball of dough after the first rising into two rectangles of 12 x 10 inches.

In a small bowl, mix the softened butter, orange zest, and sugar. Spread half of the butter mixture evenly on each rectangle. Roll up the dough, from the 12-inch side, jelly-roll style. Cut each roll into 12 slices, each about 1 inch wide. (Use a serrated knife for ease in slicing.) Place rolls into two 12-cup greased muffin tins, cut side up. Allow to rise again, covered with a tea towel in a draft-free location, for about 30 minutes. Bake on the middle rack of a preheated 375-degree-F oven for 15 to 20 minutes, until golden brown and puffed. Cool slightly before removing from pans. *Makes 24 rolls.*

Raisin Cinnamon Pecan Rolls

  1 recipe Sweet Dough (see page 91)

$1/2$ cup unsalted butter, softened

$1/4$ cup brown sugar

$1/4$ cup sugar

  1 cup golden or dark raisins
     (or a combination of both)

  1 teaspoon ground cinnamon

$3/4$ cup chopped toasted pecans

Roll out each ball of dough after the first rising into two rectangles of 12 x 10 inches.

In a small bowl, mix the softened butter, sugars, raisins, cinnamon, and pecans. Spread half of the butter mixture evenly on each rectangle. Roll up the dough, from the 12-inch side, jelly-roll style. Cut each roll into 12 slices, each about 1 inch wide. (Use a serrated knife for ease in slicing.) Place rolls into two 12-cup greased muffin tins, cut side up. Allow the dough to rise again, covered with a tea towel in a draft-free location, for about 30 minutes. Bake on the middle rack of a preheated 375-degree-F oven for 15 to 20 minutes, until golden brown and puffed. Cool slightly before removing from pans. Drizzle with icing used for the bear claws, if desired. *Makes 24 rolls.*

mini banana blueberry streusel coffee cakes

Baked in miniature cake pans, one mini cake ideally serves two with a cup of morning coffee or hot chocolate.

CRUMB TOPPING

- 3/4 cup all-purpose flour
- 1/4 cup sugar
- 4 tablespoons cold unsalted butter, cut into small pieces
- 1/4 cup chopped walnuts
- 1/2 teaspoon ground cinnamon

COFFEE CAKE

- 1 cup all-purpose flour
- 1/4 cup sugar
- 1 1/2 teaspoons baking powder
- 1/2 teaspoon baking soda
- 1 teaspoon ground cinnamon
- 1/4 teaspoon ground nutmeg
- 1/2 teaspoon kosher salt
- 1 cup fresh blueberries
- 1/4 cup chopped walnuts
- 2 large eggs
- 2 large bananas, mashed
- 1 teaspoon vanilla extract
- Powdered sugar

In a bowl, combine the flour, sugar, and butter for the topping. With a pastry cutter, cut in the butter until the size of peas. Reserve 1/2 cup of the mixture in a small bowl and add the walnuts and cinnamon; set aside.

In the bowl with the remaining flour mixture, add the first nine coffee cake ingredients.

In another bowl, beat together the eggs, bananas, and vanilla just until mixed. Add the egg mixture to the dry ingredients and stir until just combined.

Grease an 8-section mini loaf pan or a 12-cup muffin tin with Baker's Joy or vegetable spray.

Divide the batter among the individual sections. Top evenly with the reserved crumb mixture.

Bake on the middle rack of a preheated 350-degree-F oven for 35 to 40 minutes until puffed and center is set. Cool slightly before dusting with powdered sugar. *Makes 8 to 12 individual coffee cakes.*

sticky cinnamon-walnut spirals

The heady aroma of cinnamon, orange, and brown sugar is baked in one
perfect pastry. That's what this little treat offers. One bite is never enough.

½ cup dried currants

1 cup hot water

1 sheet frozen puff pastry
  (from 17.3-ounce
  package), room
  temperature

1 tablespoon butter, melted

1 teaspoon finely grated
  orange zest

½ cup finely chopped walnuts

½ cup packed dark
  brown sugar

1 teaspoon ground cinnamon

1 tablespoon butter, melted

1 tablespoon sugar

Place currants in a bowl and pour hot water over top
to cover. Steep for 15 minutes and then drain off
excess water. Cool currants to room temperature.

Roll out the pastry on a work surface. Brush the
pastry with the melted butter. Combine the orange
zest, walnuts, brown sugar, cinnamon, and reserved
currants in a bowl. Spread the mixture evenly over the
pastry. Roll up jelly-roll style, loosely. Place seam side
down and cut into 6 slices, each about 2 inches wide.

Brush the interior of the muffin tin with the
remaining tablespoon of melted butter and sprinkle
with sugar. Place the cut slices of pastry into each
muffin cup. Bake on the middle rack of a preheated
400-degree-F oven for 22 to 25 minutes until
golden brown and puffed. Allow to cool for a minute
or two before removing from muffin pan. *Serves 6.*

NOTE: This recipe can easily be doubled. Just use two
sheets of pastry, double the filling, and use a 12-cup
muffin tin.

the real deal new york crumb cake

In New York, a cup of "regular" coffee (with cream only) requires a piece of this classic crumb cake as an accompaniment. Topped with a thick layer of fragrant cinnamon buttery crumble, this recipe is as comforting a food memory as I can recall.

CRUMB CAKE

- 1 teaspoon canola oil
- 1 tablespoon all-purpose flour
- 3 cups all-purpose flour
- 1 cup sugar
- 2 tablespoons baking powder
- 1 teaspoon kosher salt
- 2 extra large eggs
- 1 cup whole milk
- 1/4 cup canola oil
- 2 teaspoons vanilla extract

CINNAMON CRUMB TOPPING

- 2 1/2 cups all-purpose flour
- 1 cup firmly packed dark brown sugar
- 2 teaspoons ground cinnamon
- 1 cup unsalted butter, melted
- Powdered sugar

Brush a 9- x 13- x 2-inch baking pan with 1 teaspoon oil and dust with 1 teaspoon flour; set aside.

In a medium bowl, combine all of the dry ingredients for the crumb cake. In another bowl, whisk all of the wet ingredients. Fold dry ingredients into wet ingredients until just combined. Do not overmix. Spread batter into the prepared baking pan.

In another medium bowl, combine the flour, brown sugar, and cinnamon for the topping; mix well. Pour the melted butter over the mixture and stir gently until large crumbs form. Sprinkle the crumbs evenly over the batter. Bake on the middle rack of a 350-degree-F oven for 25 to 27 minutes. Test with a wooden cake tester in center of cake. Sprinkle with powdered sugar when cooled to room temperature, then cut into 12 pieces and serve. *Serves 12.*

SWEETIE PIES
AND TARTS

apricot cherry tart

In July and August, fresh apricots and cherries abound in the markets. Combine these two summer fruits in a quick tart with a blush hue and bursting with flavor.

Special equipment: 8-inch diameter tart pan with removable bottom, 1 1/2 inches deep

1 (10-inch) quality store-bought pie crust (or homemade, page 118)

8 ounces cream cheese, softened

1/4 cup heavy cream

1 large egg

1/3 cup powdered sugar

1 tablespoon cornstarch

1 teaspoon finely grated orange zest

1/8 teaspoon kosher salt

4 large apricots, pitted and halved

8 fresh Bing cherries, pitted and halved

Powdered sugar

Place the pie crust into the tart pan. Chill while making the filling.

In the work bowl of a food processor or in a mixer bowl, beat the cream cheese, cream, egg, powdered sugar, cornstarch, orange zest, and salt until smooth, about 1 minute.

Place the apricots, cut side down, around the perimeter of the chilled pie crust in the tart pan. Scatter the cut cherries around the apricots and in the center of the tart. Pour the filling over the fruit. Place the tart pan on a baking sheet and bake at 350 degrees F for 45 to 50 minutes until puffed and golden.

Remove from oven; chill for 1 hour before removing outer ring of tart pan. Sprinkle with powdered sugar just before cutting. *Serves 8.*

ricotta lemon torta

Pine nuts are toasted for enhanced flavor, and along with
the addition of lemon and orange zest, form a blissful marriage.
Add creamy ricotta to the mix for a classic Sicilian dessert.

Special equipment:
two 6-inch-round
fluted tart pans with
removable bottoms

2 (10-inch) quality store-
bought pie crust (or
homemade, page 118)

2 cups (1 pound) whole
milk ricotta, drained
of excess liquid

1/2 cup heavy whipping cream

2 large egg yolks

1/3 cup sugar

Grated zest of 1 lemon
(about 1 tablespoon)

Grated zest of 1 orange
(about 1 tablespoon)

1/2 teaspoon kosher salt

1/2 cup toasted pine nuts

Powdered sugar

Press the pie crusts into the two tart pans and set
aside. In a bowl, whisk the ricotta, cream, egg yolks,
sugar, lemon zest, orange zest, and salt until smooth.
Pour the filling into prepared crusts. Sprinkle pine
nuts on top. Place the pans on a baking sheet to
prevent spills and for ease in removing from oven.
Bake on the middle rack of a preheated 375-degree-F
oven for 30 to 35 minutes until golden and filling
is set. Cool completely before taking tarts out of the
pans. Dust with powdered sugar just before serving.
Makes 8 servings.

cherry clafouti

Clafouti is a classic French dessert usually made with ruby red cherries from the overflowing wicker baskets of the village markets during summer, but other fresh fruits can be substituted. Use whatever is in season in your area.

2 tablespoons butter, softened

1 cup fresh pitted sweet cherries or 1 cup other fresh fruit (blueberries, raspberries, or sliced peaches)

2/3 cup whole milk

1/3 cup sugar

3 large eggs

1 tablespoon vanilla extract

1/8 teaspoon kosher salt

2/3 cup all-purpose flour

Powdered sugar

Whipped cream or vanilla ice cream

Butter six 6-ounce ramekins. Place the fruit in the bottom of ramekins. Place ramekins on a baking sheet for ease in moving them in and out of the oven.

In a blender, food processor, or with an electric mixer, beat the milk, sugar, eggs, vanilla, salt, and flour until the mixture is smooth, about 1 minute. Pour over the fruit and bake on the middle rack of a preheated 400-degree-F oven for 15 to 20 minutes until a knife inserted in the center comes out clean. Clafouti should be puffed when taken from oven; sprinkle with powdered sugar and serve warm with whipped cream or vanilla ice cream. *Serves 6.*

NOTE: You can substitute frozen cherries in the off-season. Thaw the cherries and drain off excess liquid.

chocolate turtle pie

Dark chocolate, pecan, and caramel all wrapped in a lovely
package of pastry. It's seductively delectable.

1 (10-inch) quality store-
   bought pie crust (or
   homemade, page 118)

1/2 cup dark corn syrup

1/2 cup firmly packed
    dark brown sugar

1/4 cup unsalted butter, melted

3 large eggs

2 teaspoons vanilla extract

2 teaspoons all-purpose flour

1/4 teaspoon kosher salt

1 cup dark chocolate bits

2 cups coarsely chopped
   toasted pecans

BOURBON WHIPPED CREAM

1 cup heavy whipping cream

1/2 cup powdered sugar

2 tablespoons bourbon
   or dark rum

Place the pie crust in a 9-inch pie pan and crimp the
edges; set aside.

In a medium bowl, whisk the corn syrup, brown
sugar, melted butter, eggs, vanilla, flour, and salt
until well combined. Stir in the chocolate and
pecans. Pour the mixture into the prepared pie
shell and bake on the middle rack of a preheated
350-degree-F oven for 45 to 50 minutes just until
the crust turns a light golden brown and the top of
the pie is firm. Remove from oven; cool for 1 hour
before slicing into 10 thin wedges.

In a mixer bowl, beat the cream with the sugar on
medium-high speed for 2 minutes, until soft peaks
form. Add the bourbon or rum and beat until stiff
peaks form, another minute on medium speed.
Refrigerate until ready to serve. Serve with Bourbon
Whipped Cream or vanilla ice cream. *Serves 10.*

chocolate caramel macadamia tart

Think pecan pie—only accentuated with macadamia nuts, mixed with chocolate and rum—all combined in a pie crust with a chocolate and caramel drizzle.

Special equipment:
9-inch tart pan with removable bottom

PIE CRUST

2 cups all-purpose flour

½ cup cold unsalted butter, cut into small pieces

½ cup cold vegetable shortening

1 teaspoon sugar

1 teaspoon kosher salt

¼ to ½ cup iced water

PIE FILLING

4 large eggs

1 cup sugar

1 cup light corn syrup

½ teaspoon kosher salt

2 teaspoons all-purpose flour

1 teaspoon vanilla extract

1 cup macadamia nuts, coarsely chopped

In the work bowl of a food processor, place the flour, butter, shortening, sugar, and salt. Pulse on and off four to five times until the butter is the size of peas.

With the motor running, add just enough iced water (no ice cubes) to form a stiff dough. This should take about 20 to 30 seconds. Do not overmix. Transfer the dough to a floured board and roll into a 6-inch disc. Chill for about 30 minutes, if time permits. Roll out to a 12-inch circle and use as desired.

Place the pie crust in the tart pan and press it up the sides.

In a bowl, beat the eggs, sugar, corn syrup, salt, flour, and vanilla until frothy. Add the nuts, chocolate, and rum. Pour mixture into the prepared pie crust. Place the tart pan on a baking sheet to prevent spillage and for ease in removing from the oven.

Bake at 350 degrees F for 50 minutes. Remove from oven; cool slightly. While the tart is cooking, make the drizzles.

1   cup dark chocolate chips

2   tablespoons dark rum

CHOCOLATE DRIZZLE
    1   cup dark chocolate chips

1/2   cup heavy cream

CARAMEL DRIZZLE
    1   cup sugar

For the Chocolate Drizzle, combine the chocolate and cream in a small saucepan. Over low heat, stir with a wooden spoon for 2 minutes until melted and smooth. With a fork, drizzle the chocolate over the baked tart in a crisscross pattern.

In another small saucepan, heat the sugar over low heat, stirring with a wooden spoon until the sugar melts and turns a caramel hue. This takes about 3 to 5 minutes. Don't get discouraged. It will turn into a liquid caramel. With a fork, drizzle the caramel over the baked tart in a crisscross pattern. Chill the tart until ready to remove the outer ring and cut into pieces. *Serves 8.*

pumpkin pecan tarts

Decadently rich, thin slices of these little tarts are all that you need,
with flavored whipped cream or ice cream, of course.

Special equipment:
six 3-inch mini tart pans

2 (10-inch) homemade pie
   crusts (page 118)

3 large eggs

1 (15-ounce) can pumpkin puree

1/2 cup sugar

1/4 cup firmly packed dark
   brown sugar

1/2 cup dark corn syrup

2 tablespoons melted butter

1 tablespoon all-purpose flour

2 teaspoons vanilla extract

3/4 teaspoon ground cinnamon

1/4 teaspoon ground nutmeg

1/4 teaspoon kosher salt

1 cup coarsely chopped pecans

TOPPING

1 cup heavy whipping cream

1/4 cup powdered sugar

1 teaspoon vanilla extract

2 tablespoons bourbon
   or dark rum

Roll the pie dough into six 4-inch circles and line the mini tart pans; crimp the edges. Place pans on baking sheets for ease in removing tarts from oven.

In a medium bowl, beat the eggs, pumpkin, sugars, corn syrup, melted butter, flour, vanilla, cinnamon, nutmeg, and salt until well combined. Pour into the prepared pie crusts. Sprinkle the pecans over top. Bake on the middle rack of a preheated 350-degree-F oven for 35 to 40 minutes until center is set. Cool for at least 1 hour before slicing; refrigerate until ready to serve.

For topping, beat the cream with powdered sugar, vanilla, and bourbon or rum until stiff peaks form. Chill until ready to serve. *Serves 6.*

classic all-american pumpkin pie with lemon-ginger cream

If you have been searching for the ultimate pumpkin pie recipe, your hunt is over. And crowned with a dollop of fragrant lemon-ginger mascarpone cream, this pie has all the makings of post-Thanksgiving dinner perfection.

1 (10-inch) homemade pie crust (page 118)

2 large eggs

1/2 cup firmly packed brown sugar

1/2 cup whipping cream

1 (15-ounce) can pumpkin puree (not pumpkin pie mix)

2 teaspoons pumpkin pie spice or 1/2 teaspoon each: cinnamon, nutmeg, cloves, and allspice

1/2 teaspoon kosher salt

1 teaspoon orange zest

LEMON-GINGER
MASCARPONE CREAM

8 ounces mascarpone cream

Juice of 1 lemon

1 teaspoon grated fresh ginger

1/4 to 1/2 cup whipping cream

Roll out the pie crust dough into a 10-inch circle. Place in an 8-inch pie pan, crimping edges. (Or use two 5-inch-round pie pans, rolling out the dough into two 6-inch circles and crimp edges.)

In a mixer, beat the eggs with sugar for 1 minute until frothy. Add the whipping cream, pumpkin, spices, salt, and orange zest. Beat another minute on low speed until the ingredients are well combined. Pour into pie crust(s). Bake at 375 degrees F until filling is set, 45 to 50 minutes for the larger pie, or 30 to 35 minutes for the smaller pies. Cool to room temperature before topping with Lemon-Ginger Mascarpone Cream.

To make the cream, whisk the ingredients until creamy, adding enough whipping cream to reach desired consistency. Refrigerate until ready to use. *Serves 8.*

lemon pine nut tart

Everything tastes better with lemon. And butter. And pine nuts. This is an all-in-one easy-to-assemble tart.

Special equipment:
9-inch tart pan with removable bottom

1 (10-inch) quality store-bought pie crust (or homemade, page 118)

3 large eggs

1/2 cup heavy cream

3/4 cup sugar

1/4 cup fresh lemon juice

1 tablespoon grated lemon zest

4 tablespoons unsalted butter, melted

1/2 teaspoon vanilla extract

1 cup toasted pine nuts

Powdered sugar

Place the pie crust in the bottom of the tart pan and press up the sides of pan. Fold any excess dough into the sides of pan.

In a medium bowl, beat the eggs, cream, and sugar until smooth. Whisk in the lemon juice, lemon zest, melted butter, vanilla, and pine nuts. Pour into the tart pan and place tart pan on a parchment-lined baking sheet. Bake on the middle rack of a 350-degree-F oven for 30 to 35 minutes or until the middle is set. Cool to room temperature, remove outer ring of tart pan, sprinkle with powdered sugar, and cut into wedges. *Serves 6 to 8.*

fresh fig mascarpone mini tarts

When fresh black mission or brown turkey figs are in season,
this tart is a must-try dessert. Figs, combined with mascarpone, lemon zest,
and honey, create the perfect balance of flavors in one bite.

CRUST

1½ cups all-purpose flour

½ cup fine cornmeal

1 tablespoon sugar

¼ teaspoon kosher salt

½ cup cold unsalted butter,
    cut into small pieces

8 tablespoons iced cold water

FILLING

½ cup sour cream

8 ounces mascarpone cheese,
    room temperature

¼ cup powdered sugar

    Zest of 1 large lemon

⅛ teaspoon kosher salt

¼ teaspoon vanilla extract

2 tablespoons red currant jelly
    or other seedless jam

2 tablespoons honey

6 large fresh black mission or
    brown turkey figs, cut into
    fourths, stems removed

¼ cup finely chopped nuts

In the work bowl of a food processor or in a bowl with a pastry cutter, combine the flour, cornmeal, sugar, salt, and butter. Pulse or cut in the butter until the mixture resembles coarse meal with pea-sized butter lumps. Drizzle with iced water and pulse or mix until just incorporated. Press the dough into a 24-cup mini tart pan, about 1 tablespoon of dough per section, pressing each halfway up the sides. Bake on the middle rack of a preheated 400-degree-F oven for 15 to 18 minutes until just golden; cool in pan.

Whisk the sour cream, mascarpone, powdered sugar, lemon zest, salt, and vanilla in a bowl. Heat the jelly or jam and honey in a small saucepan just until warmed through and the jam has melted. Place a tablespoon of filling into each of the mini tarts, top with a quarter of a fig, and brush with the jam and honey mixture. Sprinkle each tart lightly with nuts. Transfer to a serving dish. Chill until ready to serve.

Makes 24 mini tarts.

lime meringue tarts

Tart, tangy, and creamy—it's a perfect taste trio in this meringue-topped dessert. It may be a little time-consuming, but, oh, it is so worth it!

Special equipment:
2 (6-inch) tart pans with removable bottoms

1 (10-inch) quality store-bought pie crust (or homemade, page 118)

KEY LIME CURD
4 large eggs

4 large egg yolks

½ cup sugar

½ cup fresh key lime juice (from about 18 limes) or regular fresh lime juice

1 tablespoon finely grated lime zest (from about 3 key limes or 2 regular limes)

¼ teaspoon coarse kosher salt

½ cup unsalted butter, cut into ¼-inch cubes

Roll out the pie crust dough on a floured surface to fit the two 6-inch tart pans. (Roll out the dough 2 inches larger in diameter than the pans.) Press dough onto bottom and up sides of pans, then fold overhang in, forming double-thick sides extending ¼ inch above sides of pans. Pierce crusts all over with fork. Freeze crusts 20 minutes.

To make the curd, whisk the whole eggs, egg yolks, sugar, lime juice, lime zest, and salt in a medium-sized metal bowl. Set bowl over medium saucepan of simmering water (do not allow bottom of bowl to touch water). Whisk or beat with a hand mixer constantly until curd thickens slightly and an instant-read thermometer inserted into curd registers 140 degrees F, about 5 to 6 minutes total beating time (do not allow to boil). Remove bowl from over the water. Gradually whisk in butter a few cubes at a time until smooth, allowing butter cubes to melt before adding more. Chill the curd for at least 1 hour to thicken. Lime curd can be made two days ahead. Keep chilled.

Line chilled crusts with foil and then fill with dried beans or pie weights. Bake at 375 degrees F until crusts are set, about 25 minutes. Remove foil and

MERINGUE

- 4 large egg whites, room temperature
- 2/3 cup sugar
- 1/4 cup powdered sugar
- 1 teaspoon vanilla extract
- 1/4 teaspoon kosher salt

beans. Continue to bake until crusts are golden and cooked through, about 10 minutes more. Cool crusts completely in pans on rack. Spread curd evenly in baked crusts. Chill while making the meringue.

Using an electric mixer, beat the egg whites in a large bowl on medium speed until foamy. Increase speed to medium-high and beat until soft peaks form. Gradually add sugar and powdered sugar, 1 tablespoon at a time, beating until meringue is very thick and glossy, about 5 minutes. Beat in the vanilla and salt. Spoon meringue in dollops on the curd, then spread and swirl decoratively. Place the tarts on a large baking sheet and bake on the middle rack of a 400-degree-F oven for 3 to 4 minutes and then put under a medium broiler, 4 inches from heat source, for 1 minute. Chill for 1 hour before serving. Remove sides from tart pans, place tarts on platter, and serve. *Serves 12.*

pear galette with cinnamon whipped cream

A galette is a free-form tart. It's not too complicated to create, and skill in making a perfect crust is not requisite. When pears are in season, this dessert exemplifies all that is perfect in one bite.

1 (10-inch) quality store-bought pie crust (or homemade, page 118)

3 large D'Anjou or Bartlett pears, peeled, cored, thinly sliced, and fanned out

1 teaspoon ground cinnamon

1/4 teaspoon ground nutmeg

2 tablespoons sugar

1 tablespoon butter, softened

1 egg beaten with 1 tablespoon cream (egg wash)

3 tablespoons apricot preserves

CINNAMON WHIPPED CREAM

1 cup heavy whipping cream

1/4 cup powdered sugar

1 teaspoon vanilla extract

1/4 teaspoon ground cinnamon (or use 1/8 teaspoon cinnamon extract)

Place the pie crust on a baking sheet lined with parchment or Silpat. Place the sliced pears over the crust, leaving 1 1/2 inches of border around the edges. Sprinkle the pears with cinnamon, nutmeg, and sugar, and then dot the pears with butter. Fold the edges of pastry over the pears in a rustic manner. (Don't make it too perfect!) Brush the edges with the egg wash.

Bake at 400 degrees F for 25 to 30 minutes until the pastry is golden and pears are bubbly.

Heat the apricot preserves in a small saucepan over low heat just until warmed through, about 2 minutes. Remove the galette from oven; brush the top with warmed apricot preserves; cool. Cut into 6 to 8 wedges. Serve with Cinnamon Whipped Cream.

In a mixing bowl, beat the cream with the powdered sugar on medium speed until soft peaks form. Add the vanilla and cinnamon. Beat until stiff peaks form. *Serves 6 to 8.*

pâte brisée (flaky pie crust)

This dough makes two 12-inch round pie crusts
or several smaller crusts, as needed.

2 cups all-purpose flour

½ cup very cold unsalted
butter, cut into 8 pieces

½ cup very cold vegetable
shortening, cut into
small pieces

1 tablespoon sugar

¼ teaspoon kosher salt

¼ to ½ cup iced water

In the work bowl of a food processor (or use a pastry cutter in a bowl), place the flour, butter, shortening, sugar, and salt. Pulse on and off three to four times until butter and shortening have turned into pea-size pieces. Add water, a few tablespoons at a time, pulsing or mixing until a stiff dough starts to form. Do not overmix. Working the dough too much will cause a tough pastry.

Place the dough on a floured board. Divide the dough in half. Form each half into a ball; knead for a minute until combined. Chill each ball in plastic wrap for 30 minutes to 1 hour.

On a floured board, roll out each ball of dough to desired size, maximum of 12 inches per ball of dough.

three-cheese lemon pie

Combine three creamy cheeses, a smidgen of lemon curd, eggs, and ground almonds for a cheesecake-like pie with tang. The lattice top creates a lovely finish.

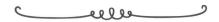

Special equipment:
8-inch diameter tart pan with removable bottom, 2 inches deep

2   (10-inch) quality store-bought pie crust (or homemade, page 118)

8   ounces goat cheese or whole milk ricotta

8   ounces mascarpone cheese

8   ounces cream cheese, softened

4   large eggs

Zest and juice of 1 lemon

2   tablespoons bottled lemon curd

½   cup finely chopped almonds

½   cup sugar

1   teaspoon vanilla extract

1   egg beaten with 1 tablespoon cream (egg wash)

2   tablespoons turbinado (raw sugar)

Powdered sugar

Place one pie crust in bottom of tart pan; set aside.

In a bowl, beat the cheeses, eggs, lemon zest and juice, lemon curd, almonds, sugar, and vanilla until well combined. Pour into the pie crust. Cut the second pie crust into 1-inch-wide strips and lay across the filling in a lattice design, making sure the lattice is loosely placed to allow the filling to rise. Brush with the egg wash, sprinkle with turbinado, and bake on a baking sheet in a 350-degree-F oven for 1 hour. Cool slightly before cutting and sprinkling with powdered sugar. *Serves 8.*

orange-glazed apple tarts

A fall sweet that subtly brightens the flavor of apples with ground
cinnamon and orange marmalade. This recipe works well with pears also.

1 package (17.3 ounces) puff
   pastry sheets, thawed

1 egg beaten with
   1 tablespoon cream
   (egg wash)

2 to 3 firm apples (Granny
   Smith, honeycrisp,
   gala) or pears
   (D'Anjou or Bartlett),
   cored and peeled

1/2 cup finely chopped
   hazelnuts, almonds,
   walnuts, pecans,
   or pine nuts

1/4 cup sugar

1 teaspoon ground cinnamon

1/2 cup orange marmalade

2 tablespoons dark
   rum (optional)

   Vanilla or seasonal ice
   cream (pumpkin, apple
   pie, or cinnamon) or
   whipped cream

Place 1 sheet of the puff pastry on a work surface and
roll out any creases. Cut the pastry into fourths. Place
the four pieces on a parchment- or Silpat-lined baking
sheet. Place the second sheet of pastry on the work
surface. Cut the pastry into eight strips lengthwise and
then cut in half horizontally to make 16 strips. Brush
the edges of each of the 4 squares with the egg wash
and then place a strip of pastry on each edge to make a
border. Brush the edges again with egg wash, and score
the edges every 1/2 inch to decorate the border.

Thinly slice the apples or pears. Place the fruit slices
on the pastry, within the border, in a decorative
pattern. Sprinkle lightly with nuts, sugar, and
cinnamon. Bake the tarts on the middle rack of a
preheated 425-degree-F oven for 15 minutes, and
then reduce heat to 375 degrees F for an additional
10 minutes. The fruit should be cooked and the
pastry golden brown and puffed. Remove from oven.

While pastry is baking, heat the marmalade and rum
in a small saucepan just until the marmalade has
melted. As soon as the pastries are removed from the
oven, brush the tops with the warmed marmalade to
form a glaze. Cool to room temperature and serve
with ice cream or whipped cream. *Serves 4.*

WARM
GOODNESS FOR
COLD DAYS

caramel apple bread pudding

This is an incredibly rich, but delicious and eye-popping dessert
for any autumn occasion. Every flavor that encapsulates the season
is in one dish—apples sautéed in butter and brown sugar, croissants
and custard to make a bread pudding filling, a freshly baked
pumpkin—served with caramel sauce and ice cream. The recipe can
be cut in half, if desired; just use the pumpkin only instead of the
pumpkin and the individual baking dishes for extra pudding.

1   (8-inch) diameter
    fresh pumpkin

¼   cup water

6   large eggs

2   cups half-and-half

1   cup sour cream

6   large croissants

4   tablespoons unsalted
    butter

1   large or 2 medium
    apples (Granny Smith,
    honeycrisp), cored
    and thinly sliced

½   cup brown sugar

½   cup chopped dried
    apricots

½   cup raisins or craisins

½   cup chopped nuts of
    choice (pecans, almonds,
    walnuts, or hazelnuts)

Cut enough off the top (leaving the base alone) of
the pumpkin so that there is an opening of at least
6 inches across, and clean out the seeds. Place the
water in the pumpkin, cover with plastic wrap, and
microwave for 5 minutes. Remove water and pat dry.

In a large bowl, beat the eggs, half-and-half, and sour
cream until smooth. Break the croissants into 1-inch
pieces; add to egg mixture.

In a medium skillet, heat the butter and sauté the
apple slices for 2 to 3 minutes. Add the brown
sugar, apricots, raisins, nuts, pumpkin pie spice,
and salt. Sauté another 2 to 3 minutes until sugar
is melted. Cool to room temperature and then add
to the egg and croissant mixture; stir well. (This
can be done hours ahead, or even the night before,
then refrigerated.) Pour enough mixture into
the pumpkin to come to within 1 inch of the top,
and place the remaining bread pudding in several
buttered individual baking dishes. Wrap the pumpkin

(continued)

caramel apple bread pudding (cont.)

2 teaspoons pumpkin
   pie spice

½ teaspoon kosher salt

TOPPING

1 cup bottled caramel sauce

½ cup whipping cream

   Vanilla ice cream or
   whipped cream
   (optional)

loosely in foil and place on a baking sheet. Place a sheet of foil over the extra baking dishes of pudding and bake both on the middle rack of a 375-degree-F oven for 1 hour; remove foil from both the pumpkin and the baking dishes and bake an additional 15 minutes. Remove from oven; cool the stuffed pumpkin at least 30 minutes before slicing.

Heat the caramel sauce and cream in a small saucepan. Cut the pumpkin into 8 wedges, lay each slice on its side, top with some of the caramel sauce, and serve with ice cream or whipped cream. Use the extra bread pudding for another night or for guests who don't like pumpkin or squash, or use it as a filling for a second smaller pumpkin. *Serves 12 to 16.*

NOTE: Another option that is time-consuming but impressive is to carve out 12 mini pumpkins to use as the baking "vessels." Bake the mini pumpkins for about 35 minutes, rather than the hour for the large pumpkin. There is no need to microwave first since the pumpkins are so small and not as meaty as a large pumpkin.

handheld fruit pies

Store-bought puff pastry and fresh berries combine to
create a pie that is easy to eat with one hand.

2 sheets (17.3-ounce
   package) frozen puff
   pastry, thawed

1 cup blueberries

1 cup blackberries

½ cup sugar

2 tablespoons cornstarch

½ teaspoon kosher salt

½ teaspoon cinnamon

4 ounces cream cheese,
   cut into 8 pieces

1 egg beaten with
   1 tablespoon cream
   (egg wash)

2 tablespoons turbinado
   (raw sugar)

Place the 2 sheets of puff pastry on a work surface.
Roll out any creases in the dough. Cut each into
fourths so you have 8 squares; set aside.

In a bowl, combine the blueberries, blackberries,
sugar, cornstarch, salt, and cinnamon; toss gently.
Place a piece of cream cheese in the center of
each square. Top each with equal amounts of the
fruit mixture. Fold the dough over filling into an
envelope. With a fork, crimp the edges to prevent any
fruit from spilling out. Transfer to a baking sheet
and brush with the egg wash, then sprinkle with the
turbinado. Cut three little slits on top of each fruit
pie. Bake in a 425-degree-F oven for 15 minutes
until pastry is golden and puffed. Cool slightly before
serving. *Serves 8.*

warm espresso cakes

You can easily prepare these ahead, and then bake as
needed. The finished product is warm and gooey with
a hint of coffee along with the dark chocolate.

2 tablespoons unsalted
   butter, softened

2 tablespoons sugar

6 ounces semisweet or
   bittersweet chocolate,
   coarsely chopped

12 tablespoons unsalted
   butter

2 tablespoons instant
   espresso crystals

3 large whole eggs

4 large egg yolks

1½ cups powdered sugar

½ cup all-purpose flour

   Sliced strawberries or fresh
   raspberries, powdered
   sugar, ice cream

Place six 6-ounce ramekins on a baking sheet and rub
the inside of each with the 2 tablespoons butter and
then sprinkle with sugar; set aside.

In a medium saucepan, heat the chocolate with
12 tablespoons butter and espresso until melted.
Cool slightly and then in a medium bowl, whisk the
whole eggs and egg yolks until frothy. Whisk in the
melted chocolate, powdered sugar, and flour. Pour
into the prepared ramekins, dividing batter equally.
(The recipe can be made ahead up to this point, then
refrigerated until ready to bake.)

Bake at 450 degrees F for 12 to 15 minutes on
the middle rack of oven. Cakes should be cooked
through, not runny in the center. Remove from
oven and let cakes cool slightly before removing
from ramekins by running a knife around the edges
to loosen. Turn onto a serving plate, dust with
powdered sugar, and serve with fresh berries and ice
cream. *Serves 6.*

sticky date pudding with warm pecan-toffee sauce

Is there a better sweet treat combination than dates, ginger, cinnamon, and pecans? Warmed miniature cakes, topped with pecan-toffee sauce and with the added goodness of whipped cream or ice cream, makes this dessert full of comfort and joy all year round.

2 cups coarsely chopped pitted dried dates

2 cups water

1½ teaspoons baking soda

1 tablespoon crystallized ginger or 1 teaspoon ground ginger

2 cups all-purpose flour

½ teaspoon baking powder

½ teaspoon kosher salt

1 teaspoon vanilla extract

½ cup unsalted butter, softened

1 cup sugar

3 large eggs

In a medium saucepan, simmer the dates in the water for 5 minutes over medium heat. Remove the pan from heat and stir in the baking soda and ginger over a sink in case the mixture starts to foam and overflow. Let the mixture stand for 20 minutes, stirring occasionally. It will become thicker as it sits.

While the mixture is standing, combine the flour, baking powder, and salt in a bowl. In a mixer bowl, beat the vanilla, butter, and sugar until light and fluffy. Beat in the eggs, one at a time. Add the flour mixture, gradually. Slowly stir in the date mixture until just combined. Do not overmix.

Spray and flour eight 6-ounce ramekins. (There might be enough batter for 9 or 10 ramekins, so spray and flour a few extra if you like.) Pour enough batter into each ramekin to fill three-fourths full. Place the ramekins in a baking pan with sides and fill the pan with hot water until water is halfway up the sides of the ramekins.

WARM PECAN-TOFFEE SAUCE

6 tablespoons unsalted butter

3/4 cup dark brown sugar

1 teaspoon ground cinnamon

1/4 cup half-and-half

1 cup chopped pecans

Vanilla ice cream or whipped cream

Bake on the middle rack of a 375-degree-F oven for 45 to 50 minutes until center of pudding is set (test with a wooden skewer—if it comes out clean, they are done). Remove from oven, take ramekins out of the water, and cool.

In a small saucepan, heat the butter, brown sugar, cinnamon, half-and-half, and pecans. Stir over low heat until the sauce is thickened, about 3 to 5 minutes.

Invert each cooled pudding onto a serving dish and top with some of the sauce. Serve with a scoop of vanilla ice cream or whipped cream. *Serves 8–10.*

hot fudge pudding cake

Warm and comforting, this dessert combines the rich goodness
of chocolate with the consistency of an ooey gooey cake.

1   cup all-purpose flour

3/4   cup sugar

2   tablespoons baking cocoa

2   teaspoons baking powder

1/4   teaspoon kosher salt

1/2   cup milk

1   teaspoon vanilla extract

2   tablespoons butter, melted

1/4   cup chopped nuts
     (optional)

1   cup light brown sugar

1/4   teaspoon kosher salt

1/4   cup baking cocoa

2   teaspoons vanilla extract

1 3/4   cups hot water

   Vanilla ice cream or
   whipped cream

Measure the flour, sugar, 2 tablespoons cocoa, baking
powder, and 1/4 teaspoon salt into a mixing bowl.
Stir in milk, 1 teaspoon vanilla, and melted butter;
blend in nuts if using. Spread batter in an ungreased
9-inch-square pan.

Stir together the brown sugar, 1/4 teaspoon salt, and
1/4 cup cocoa; sprinkle over batter. Stir 2 teaspoons
vanilla into hot water and pour gently over all. Bake
at 350 degrees F for 45 minutes. Serve warm with
sweetened whipped cream or ice cream. *Serves 9.*

warmed figs with cambozola and hazelnuts

When fresh figs are in season—July to October—and just a
little sweet indulgence is required, combine the distinctive taste and
texture of a fig with the creaminess of blue cheese, sweetness of honey,
and crunchiness of nuts for a "pop-in-your-mouth" sensation.

8 to 12 brown turkey or
    black mission figs

¼ pound soft blue cheese,
    such as Cambozola

¼ cup crushed hazelnuts

2 tablespoons honey

    Ground black pepper

2 to 3 tablespoons chopped
    fresh rosemary

Cut figs in half lengthwise and place on a baking
pan. Top each with a small dollop of cheese and a
few chopped nuts. Bake at 400 degrees F for 5 to
8 minutes until cheese melts slightly. Serve warm
drizzled with honey, a grind or two of black pepper,
and the fresh rosemary. *Makes about 16 fig bites.*

cinnamon caramel crumble

This crumble captures the flavors of an autumn day at the
farmstand—apples and pears—baked with citrus and caramely
brown sugar and topped with a crunchy cinnamon layer.
It's a perfect fall confection craving satisfaction.

FILLING

4   Granny Smith apples, peeled,
      cored, and thinly sliced

2   D'Anjou pears, peeled,
      cored, and thinly sliced

    Juice and zest of 1 lemon

3/4   cup brown sugar

3   tablespoons unsalted butter,
      cut into small pieces

2   tablespoons cornstarch

1   teaspoon kosher salt

CRUMBLE TOPPING

1   cup all-purpose flour

1   cup quick-cooking oats

4   tablespoons unsalted butter,
      cut into small pieces

1   cup chopped walnuts

1/4   cup brown sugar

1   teaspoon ground cinnamon

    Vanilla ice cream or
      whipped cream

Combine the apples, pears, lemon juice and zest,
sugar, butter, cornstarch, and salt in a bowl and mix
well; transfer to eight individual baking dishes or
1-cup ramekins.

In a bowl, combine all topping ingredients except the
ice cream and crumble with your hands or a pastry
cutter to make sure it is well mixed. Pour over the
prepared fruits. Bake in a preheated 375-degree-F
oven for 30 to 35 minutes until bubbly and golden
brown. Serve topped with vanilla ice cream or
whipped cream. *Serves 8.*

deconstructed apple tart tatin

Tart Tatin is a traditional French dessert, most often baked in a pan, then inverted. This version has all the components cooked separately, then combined to create a tower of delicious flavors.

2   tablespoons butter

1   cup sugar

4   large Granny Smith apples, peeled, cored, and thinly sliced

1   sheet store-bought frozen puff pastry (17.3 ounce package), thawed and rolled out

2   tablespoons turbinado (raw sugar)

HONEY LAVENDER CREAM

2   cups heavy whipping cream

½   cup powdered sugar

1   teaspoon culinary lavender

2   tablespoons honey

In an ovenproof 8- or 9-inch skillet, heat the butter and add sugar. Cook over low heat until the sugar starts to melt, and then stir with a wooden spoon or heat-resistant spatula. Continue to cook until the mixture starts to turn light brown and smooth in texture. Do not overcook. The sugar will reach caramel stage in about 3 to 4 minutes; cool slightly and then add the apples. Transfer skillet to oven and bake at 375 degrees F for 15 minutes. Toss to coat the apples with caramel after the first 7 or 8 minutes of baking. Remove from oven when apples are cooked through; cool slightly.

Roll out the pastry on a work surface and use a 3-inch-round scalloped biscuit cutter or other various shaped 3-inch cookie cutters (leaves, teapots, stars, and so on) and place the cutout pastry on a Silpat- or parchment-lined baking sheet. Sprinkle with the turbinado. Bake on the middle rack of a preheated 425-degree-F oven for 15 to 20 minutes until the pastry is puffed and golden brown.

(continued)

deconstructed apple tart tatin (cont.)

While the pastry is baking, prepare the cream. In a mixer bowl, beat the whipping cream on medium speed for 2 minutes until it starts to thicken. Add the sugar, lavender, and honey. Beat until stiff peaks form. Chill until ready to serve.

To serve, place a spoonful of warm apples in a serving dish. Top with one or two warm puff pastry cutouts. Serve with a dollop of Honey Lavender Cream on top or on the side. *Serves 4 to 6.*

summer peach cobbler

Succulent freshly picked peaches, white or yellow, in mid-August, combine
with citrus and spices to create an exquisite cobbler with a buttery crust.

FILLING

8 large peaches, pitted
and sliced into ¼-inch-
thick slices (about
8 to 10 cups fruit)

Zest and juice of 1 lemon

1 teaspoon ground cinnamon

½ teaspoon ground nutmeg

¾ cup sugar

¼ cup brown sugar

1 tablespoon cornstarch

1 teaspoon kosher salt

COBBLER CRUST

2 cups all-purpose flour

½ cup cold unsalted butter,
cut into 8 small pieces

1 tablespoon sugar

1 teaspoon kosher salt

1 teaspoon baking powder

1 to 1½ cups half-and-half

Turbinado (raw sugar)
or sanding sugar

Combine all filling ingredients in a bowl, toss well,
and spoon into a 9- x 13-inch baking pan.

In another bowl, combine the flour and butter and
crumble with a pastry cutter or your fingers until
butter is the size of small peas. Add the sugar, salt,
baking powder, and enough half-and-half to make a
soft dough. Drop 9 to 12 little dollops of dough over
the fruit and then lightly sprinkle with turbinado.
Bake at 375 degrees F for 45 minutes until dough is
golden and the filling is bubbly. *Serves 9 to 12.*

NOTE: You can make individual cobblers using eight
1-cup ramekins, baking at 375 degrees F for 35 to 40
minutes, until cobbler is golden and filling is bubbly.

individual blackberry-apricot cobblers

Berries and apricots are both perfect alone, but are even more delectable when mixed in a spice-infused filling and topped with a crispy cobbler crust.

FRUIT FILLING

- 2 cups blackberries
- 6 apricots, pitted and cut into ½-inch-thick slices (to make about 4 cups)
- 1 tablespoon cornstarch
- ½ cup sugar
- ½ teaspoon ground cinnamon
- ¼ teaspoon ground nutmeg
- ½ teaspoon kosher salt
- Juice and zest of 1 lemon

COBBLER CRUST

- 2 cups all-purpose flour
- ½ cup cold unsalted butter, cut into 8 small pieces
- 1 tablespoon sugar
- 1 teaspoon kosher salt
- 1 teaspoon baking powder
- 1 to 1½ cups half-and-half
- Turbinado (raw sugar) or sanding sugar

Combine all ingredients for the fruit filling in a bowl; toss well. Spoon into eight 1-cup ramekins.

In another bowl, combine the flour and butter and crumble with a pastry cutter or your fingers until butter is the size of small peas. Add the sugar, salt, baking powder, and enough half-and-half to make a soft dough. Drop dollops of dough over the fruit and then sprinkle lightly with the turbinado. Place the filled ramekins on a baking sheet to prevent spills.

Bake the cobblers on the middle rack of a 375-degree-F oven for 35 to 40 minutes until cobbler is golden and filling is bubbly. *Serves 8.*

whidbey island berry buckle

Every summer, I have the pleasure of spending time on picturesque Whidbey Island. It's a culinary haven for mussels, Dungeness crab, lavender, and, in summer months, the most succulent berries on earth. The farmers markets on the island always have berry vendors with winding lines of patient customers waiting for freshly picked loganberries, marionberries, tayberries, blueberries, blackberries, strawberries, and raspberries.

BATTER

- ¼ cup unsalted butter, softened
- ½ cup sugar
- 1 large egg
- 1 teaspoon vanilla extract
- 1 teaspoon finely grated orange zest
- 1 cup all-purpose flour
- 1 teaspoon baking powder
- ¼ teaspoon kosher salt
- ⅓ cup heavy cream
- 4 cups mixed berries (blackberries, blueberries, strawberries, raspberries, marionberries, tayberries, or loganberries)

For the batter, beat the butter and sugar in the bowl of a mixer with the paddle attachment for 2 to 3 minutes until light in color and fluffy. Add the egg, vanilla, and orange zest. Beat for 1 minute until combined. Mix the flour, baking powder, and salt in a small bowl. Slowly add to the wet ingredients, beating just until mixed, and then add the cream until the mixture forms a batter, about 1 minute on medium speed. Divide the batter among six ramekins (or 8 ramekins to make smaller portions). Divide the mixed berries among the ramekins, filling each to about three-fourths full; set aside.

TOPPING

¼ cup unsalted butter, cold
     and cut into small pieces

½ cup sugar

½ teaspoon ground cinnamon

¼ teaspoon ground nutmeg

⅓ cup all-purpose flour

    Whipped cream or
     vanilla ice cream

For the topping, combine the butter, sugar, cinnamon, nutmeg, and flour. With a pastry cutter (or a food processor), blend until the butter is the size of small peas. Divide the mixture among the ramekins, spreading evenly over the top of each. Pat the crumble mixture down slightly.

Place the ramekins on a parchment-lined baking sheet with sides. Bake on the middle rack at 375 degrees F for 40 minutes. If topping is not crisp enough after baking time, place under a low broiler for about 30 seconds to crisp up slightly, but no more than 30 seconds, otherwise it will burn. Remove from oven and cool to room temperature. Serve with whipped cream or vanilla ice cream.
Serves 6 to 8.

WHEN
CRAVING
CAKES

buttercream frosting

For the final touch on any cake or cupcake, this frosting is as easy
as can be. Within minutes, a topping of your choice can be created
with the addition of food coloring, extracts, or cocoa powder.

½ cup unsalted butter,
   room temperature

2½ cups powdered sugar

1 teaspoon vanilla extract

In a mixer bowl, beat the butter and sugar for 2 to 3
minutes on medium speed until smooth.

Add vanilla extract and beat another 30 seconds. Use
as a vanilla buttercream frosting.

NOTE: For different flavorings, add 1 tablespoon
cocoa powder for chocolate frosting or try 1 teaspoon
lemon extract and a drop of yellow food coloring for
lemon frosting. Add other food coloring, a drop at a
time, until the tint of the frosting is to your liking.

chocolate brownie mascarpone trifle with berries

With mascarpone and berries, these brownie bites are delicious.

8 ounces mascarpone cheese, softened

1 cup heavy whipping cream

1/2 cup powdered sugar

1 teaspoon vanilla extract

2 cups fresh raspberries

2 cups fresh blueberries

1/4 cup sugar

1 pound chocolate brownie bites (found in the bakery of most markets)

In a mixer bowl, beat the mascarpone cheese with the heavy cream, powdered sugar, and vanilla until semi-stiff. Don't overbeat, otherwise you will not be able to spread.

Combine the raspberries, blueberries, and sugar in a medium bowl. Place a few brownie pieces (about 4) in individual goblets. Spread some of the cream over the brownies and top with a few tablespoons of berries. Repeat layers; cover and refrigerate until ready to serve. *Serves 8.*

NOTE: Drizzle just the bottom layer of each of the goblets of brownies with a tablespoon of Godiva Chocolate Liqueur for an added depth in flavor.

NOTE: One recipe homemade brownies, cut into 3/4-inch pieces (about 64 bites total) can be used in place of the brownie bites.

chocolate cupcake surprise with lemon cream cheese frosting

The rich chocolate combines well with the tangy lemon frosting.

3/4 cup unsweetened
      cocoa powder

3/4 cup all-purpose flour

1/2 teaspoon baking powder

1/4 teaspoon kosher salt

3/4 cup unsalted butter, softened

1 cup sugar

3 large eggs

1 teaspoon vanilla extract

1/2 cup sour cream

12 miniature marshmallows

LEMON CREAM CHEESE FROSTING

8 ounces cream cheese, softened

4 ounces unsalted
      butter, softened

1/2 cup powdered sugar

1 tablespoon lemon extract

  Drop of food coloring
  (optional)

2 cups toasted flaked coconut

Line a muffin tin with 12 paper cupcake liners; set aside.

In a medium bowl, combine the cocoa powder, flour, baking powder, and salt.

In a mixing bowl, cream the butter and sugar until fluffy. Add the eggs, one at a time, to the butter mixture. Beat in the vanilla and sour cream and then slowly add the dry ingredients. Do not overbeat. Pour about 1 tablespoon batter into the muffin tins, place 1 miniature marshmallow in center, and then top with more batter until three-fourths full. Bake at 350 degrees F for 20 minutes. Remove from oven; cool slightly.

In a mixer bowl, beat the cream cheese, butter, powdered sugar, lemon extract, and food coloring, if using, until smooth. Spread each cupcake with some of the frosting. Place the coconut in a bowl. Dip each frosted cupcake in the coconut to coat. *Makes 12 cupcakes.*

NOTE: If coconut is not your favorite topping, substitute colored candies, sprinkles, or shaved chocolate.

chocolate orange cake with chocolate ganache

I hardly ever use packaged cake mixes, but for ease and convenience, this recipe is enhanced with a soupçon of coffee liqueur and orange zest. With the drizzle of chocolate ganache, the cake looks professionally made. And unless the cook confesses, the secret of this spectacular dessert is safe. Sometimes, shortcuts are justifiable!

1   package devil's food
      chocolate cake mix

8   ounces sour cream

1   package (4 ounces)
      instant chocolate
      fudge pudding mix

4   large eggs

½   cup vegetable oil

½   cup cold water

¼   cup coffee liqueur (Kahlua)

2   tablespoons finely
      grated orange zest

CHOCOLATE GANACHE

12 ounces semisweet
      chocolate chips

1   cup heavy cream

     Orange zest strips

Place all ingredients for cake in the bowl of a mixer and beat on medium speed for 3 minutes. Pour into a greased and floured 10-inch Bundt pan or a 9- x 13- x 3-inch baking pan. Bake on the middle rack of a preheated 350-degree-F oven for about 55 to 60 minutes for the Bundt pan or 45 to 50 minutes for the baking pan. Bake until center is set. Test with a wooden pick (if pick comes out clean, the cake is done; if it comes out slightly wet, bake the cake for a few more minutes). Allow cake to cool in pan before turning out onto a cake platter.

In a small saucepan, combine the chocolate chips and cream; stir over low heat for 3 minutes until mixture is warmed through and chocolate is thick and shiny. Cool slightly and then pour over cake. With a silicone brush, spread the ganache evenly over cake; sprinkle with orange zest strips and cool in refrigerator so that the ganache can harden. *Serves 8 to 10.*

NOTE: I use a pan of miniature cake molds with twenty flower-shaped designs when doing these for a luncheon or buffet. I have enough batter for about 36 miniature cakes, using the mold twice. Just bake for about 25 minutes for the miniature cakes.

chocolate stout cake

Dark chocolate is combined with dark stout in a moist batter for a cake to savor. Topped with ganache, it's the ideal chocolate treat. Make it into three individual cakes or into smaller cakes in muffin tins or decorative molds.

2 cups oatmeal stout, Guinness, or Murphy's Dry Irish (nitrogenated stout)

2 cups unsalted butter

1½ cups unsweetened cocoa powder (preferably Dutch process)

4 cups all-purpose flour

2 cups sugar

1 tablespoon baking soda

1½ teaspoons kosher salt

4 large eggs

1⅓ cups sour cream

CHOCOLATE GANACHE

12 ounces semisweet chocolate chips

1 cup heavy cream

Coffee, chocolate mint, or vanilla ice cream

Butter three 8-inch-round cake pans and line with parchment paper; butter the paper. Bring the stout and butter to a simmer in a large, heavy saucepan over medium heat. Add cocoa powder and whisk until mixture is smooth; cool slightly.

Whisk the flour, sugar, baking soda, and salt in a large bowl to blend. Using an electric mixer, beat the eggs and sour cream in another large bowl to blend. Add the stout-chocolate mixture to egg mixture and beat just to combine. Add the flour mixture and beat briefly on slow speed. Using a rubber spatula, fold batter until completely combined. Divide batter equally among prepared pans. Bake cakes at 350 degrees F until tester inserted into center of cakes comes out clean, about 35 minutes. Transfer cakes to a wire rack; cool 10 minutes. Turn cakes out onto rack and cool completely.

In a small saucepan, combine the chocolate chips and cream; stir over low heat for 3 minutes until mixture is warmed through and chocolate is thick and shiny. Cool slightly and then pour over cakes. With a silicone brush, spread the ganache evenly over cakes. Cool in refrigerator so that the ganache can harden. *Serves 8 to 10.*

chocolate zucchini cake

Vegetables never tasted so scrumptious! Sneak zucchini in a cake and, mixed with chocolate, moistness is guaranteed.

4 large eggs

1½ cups canola oil

1½ cups sugar

3 cups finely grated raw zucchini (unpeeled)

3 cups all-purpose flour

1½ teaspoons baking powder

1 teaspoon baking soda

2 teaspoons ground cinnamon

1 teaspoon kosher salt

1 cup chopped walnuts, pecans, or almonds

2 squares (2 ounces) unsweetened chocolate, melted

Powdered sugar, ice cream, or chocolate ganache (page 148) (optional)

In a bowl of a mixer, beat the eggs until creamy and light yellow, about 3 minutes on medium speed. Add the oil and sugar and beat another 2 minutes. Add the zucchini, flour, baking powder, baking soda, cinnamon, salt, nuts, and melted chocolate. Beat for 1 minute on medium speed until just combined. Pour batter into a greased and floured 12-cup Bundt pan. Bake on the middle rack of a preheated 350-degree-F oven for about 75 minutes. Cool in pan for 10 minutes before turning out and serve with powdered sugar, ice cream, or ganache. *Makes 1 large Bundt cake.*

NOTE: You can also bake these in two 6-cup Bundt pans for about 45 minutes at 350 degrees F, or individual 2-cup Bundt pans for about 30 to 35 minutes. Or try baking them in decorative muffin-sized tins for cute cakes. Bake for about 30 to 35 minutes or until center is cooked through when tested with a wooden pick. Again, cool cakes 10 minutes before turning out onto serving platter and serve with your choice of toppings.

strawberry tiramisu

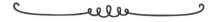

This classic Italian *tiramisu* "pick me up," dessert has a summer twist
with the addition of berries. Easy to assemble in layers as a trifle-style
sweet, allow the tiramisu to set up for a few hours before serving. This
dessert can be assembled in one large bowl or in individual servings.

16   ounces mascarpone
       cheese, softened

  1   cup heavy whipping cream

½   cup powdered sugar

¼   cup sweet Marsala

  2   cups strong espresso
       coffee

¼   cup sugar

½   cup Kahlua (coffee-
       flavored liqueur)

36   firm Italian ladyfinger
       biscuits

  1   quart fresh strawberries,
       hulled and thinly sliced

  1   tablespoon cocoa powder
       mixed with ¼ cup
       powdered sugar

In the bowl of a mixer, beat the mascarpone, cream,
and powdered sugar for 1 minute on medium speed.
Slowly add the Marsala. The mixture should be soft,
smooth, and spreadable.

In a bowl, whisk the espresso, sugar, and Kahlua.
Place 18 of the ladyfingers in a single layer on the
bottom of a decorative 9- x 13- x 2-inch baking dish
or glass bowl, or put 2 ladyfingers on the bottom
of goblets (you might have to break them in half).
Brush the ladyfingers with half of the espresso
mixture. Place half of the mascarpone mixture
on the ladyfingers. Divide the berries among the
ladyfingers or place half on the ladyfingers in the
baking dish. Place the remaining ladyfingers on the
berries. Brush with remaining coffee mixture, using
all the coffee. Top with remaining mascarpone cream
and place the strawberries decoratively on top.

Cover loosely with plastic wrap. Refrigerate until
ready to serve. Chill at least 3 hours and up to 24
hours. Cut the tiramisu in the baking pan into
12 serving pieces. Sprinkle the serving platter or
individual goblets lightly with the cocoa powder
mixture just before serving. *Serves 9 to 12.*

fresh peach brûlée cheesecake

With a glimmer of thinly sliced peaches on top, this cheesecake
sums up all that is summer in one bite. Easy yet show
stopping, a mini cheesecake will serve 6 small portions.

Special equipment:
a 5 1/2-inch springform
pan, 2 1/2 inches deep

CRUST

1 cup ground almond biscotti

2 tablespoons melted butter

FILLING

8 ounces cream cheese,
softened

1/2 cup sour cream

1/4 teaspoon almond extract

1 cup coarsely chopped
peeled fresh peaches

1/4 cup sugar

1 large egg

1 tablespoon cornstarch

1/8 teaspoon kosher salt

TOPPING

1 white or yellow peach,
pitted and sliced
into 16 thin slices

2 tablespoons sugar

1 large raspberry, blueberry,
or blackberry

Combine the biscotti and melted butter in a bowl.
Press the mixture onto the bottom and 1/2 inch up the
sides of the springform pan.

In the work bowl of a food processor, beat the
cream cheese, sour cream, almond extract, peaches,
sugar, egg, cornstarch, and salt until smooth, about
1 minute. Pour into the prepared springform pan.

Wrap the bottom of the pan with aluminum foil.
Place the pan into a larger baking pan and fill halfway
up the sides with warm water (this is called a "bain-
marie"). Bake on the middle rack of a preheated
350-degree-F oven for 55 to 60 minutes until center
is set. Remove from oven; chill completely.

Preheat the broiler and place the oven rack 4 inches
from the heat source. Place the sliced peaches in a
concentric circle on the cheesecake. Sprinkle lightly
with the sugar. Place a berry in the center of the
peaches. Broil the cake for 1 minute, just until the
sugar starts to bubble and turn a light brown. Remove
from oven; chill again for 1 hour before removing the
outer ring of the springform pan to serve. *Serves 6.*

italian cassata

If you are a confident baker, this rum-soaked sponge cake recipe is for you. This is the classic cake of Sicily. Cassata with a ricotta filling are in every *pasticceria*. Pistachio nuts and ricotta are found in many Sicilian pastries.

SPONGECAKE

- 6 large egg whites, room temperature
- 1/2 teaspoon cream of tartar
- 1/8 teaspoon kosher salt
- 2 tablespoons sugar
- 6 large egg yolks, room temperature
- 2 tablespoons sugar
- 1/8 teaspoon kosher salt
- 2 teaspoons cornstarch
- 1/4 cup unsalted butter, melted and cooled
- 1/4 cup very finely chopped pistachios
- 1/4 cup dark rum
- 1 tablespoon sugar

In a mixer bowl, beat the egg whites with cream of tartar and salt until thickened, about 3 minutes. While still beating, slowly add the sugar until the egg whites are stiff; set aside in a bowl.

In another mixer bowl, beat the egg yolks, 2 tablespoons sugar, and salt until thick and creamy, about 5 to 8 minutes. Add the cornstarch and beat another minute. Slowly add the cooled melted butter and pistachios. Fold the egg whites into the egg yolk mixture.

Divide the batter between two 8-inch-square cake pans that have been lined with parchment paper and sprayed with vegetable oil or nonstick cooking spray. Bake on the middle rack of a 350-degree-F oven for about 18 to 20 minutes until just lightly browned. Cool for 30 minutes in pan. Turn out onto a wire rack and remove the parchment paper.

Combine the rum and 1 tablespoon sugar in a small bowl; set aside.

(continued)

italian cassata (cont.)

RICOTTA FILLING

- 1 pound whole milk ricotta
- 1/2 cup powdered sugar
- 1 teaspoon vanilla extract
- 2 drops cinnamon oil or 1/2 teaspoon cinnamon extract
- 1 teaspoon finely grated orange zest
- 1/2 cup mini chocolate chips (regular size are too big)

TOPPING

- 1 1/2 cups heavy whipping cream
- 1/4 cup powdered sugar
- 1 teaspoon vanilla extract
- 1/4 cup grated dark chocolate
- 1/4 cup finely chopped pistachios
- Powdered sugar

In a mixer bowl, beat the ricotta, powdered sugar, vanilla, cinnamon oil or extract, and orange zest until smooth, about 1 minute on medium speed. Stir in the chocolate chips and mix well.

In another mixer bowl, beat the cream with the powdered sugar and vanilla until stiff peaks form. Reserve the grated chocolate and pistachios for garnishing.

Place one of the cakes on a serving platter that has been sprinkled with powdered sugar to prevent the cake from sticking to the plate. With a pastry brush, brush the cake with half of the rum mixture. Spread the ricotta mixture evenly on the cake to about 3/4 inch thickness. Top with second cake layer. Brush with remaining rum mixture.

Using a pastry bag or with an off-set spreader, spread the whipped cream on the top and sides of the cake. Or, cut the cake into 9 to 12 pieces and spread the cream on each individual square.

Sprinkle tops with chocolate and pistachios. *Serves 9 to 12.*

NOTE: The ricotta filling can also be used in cannoli as shown in picture. Using a pastry bag fitted with a 1-inch tip, pipe the filling into miniature- or regular-sized cannoli shells that can be purchased in many Italian delis. Sprinkle with powdered sugar and dip ends in crushed pistachios.

italian plum almond cake

In midsummer, when plums are literally dropping from trees, an almond-flavored cake dotted with fresh plums is the solution for the abundance of plums at your fingertips.

1½ cups all-purpose flour

2 teaspoons baking powder

½ teaspoon kosher salt

½ teaspoon almond extract

1 large egg

¾ cup sugar

½ cup whole milk

¼ cup vegetable oil

12 Italian plums, pitted and cut in half

TOPPING

1 tablespoon brown sugar

½ cup sliced almonds

2 tablespoons all-purpose flour

¼ teaspoon ground cinnamon

1 tablespoon cold unsalted butter, cut into small pieces

Powdered sugar

In a medium-size bowl, whisk together the flour, baking powder, and salt; set aside.

In a separate bowl, combine the almond extract, egg, sugar, milk, and oil; whisk until smooth. Fold the wet mixture into the flour mixture and stir until just blended. Spoon the batter into a greased 9-inch-round cake pan and smooth out the top. Arrange the plum halves, cut side down, over the batter.

Combine the brown sugar, almonds, flour, cinnamon, and butter and sprinkle the mixture over the plums. Bake at 375 degrees F on the middle rack of the oven until the top of the cake is golden, the plums are soft, and a toothpick inserted into the center of the cake comes out clean, about 35 to 40 minutes. Cool slightly before serving with powdered sugar sprinkled on top. *Serves 6 to 8.*

mini new york cheesecakes

Lemon, cream cheese, and sour cream combined in a decadent confection epitomizes all that is perfect in a dessert. For those of us who look for the lemon/cream combination on dessert menus above all else, it's nirvana.

CRUST

1½ cups graham cracker crumbs

¼ cup ground almonds

½ teaspoon ground cinnamon

4 tablespoons butter, melted

FILLING

24 ounces cream cheese, softened

2 cups sour cream

1 heaping tablespoon cornstarch

4 large eggs

¾ cup sugar

1 teaspoon lemon extract

Zest of 1 large lemon

2 tablespoons butter, melted

¼ teaspoon kosher salt

LEMON GLAZE

¾ cup bottled lemon curd

¼ cup water

1 teaspoon cornstarch

Zest of 1 large lemon

In a bowl, combine the crumbs, almonds, cinnamon, and melted butter. Spread the mixture into the bottoms of two 6-inch-round springform pans.

In a food processor, combine all of the filling ingredients and blend with a metal blade for 5 minutes until smooth. Pour into the prepared pans and place on a baking sheet. Bake in a preheated 425-degree-F oven for 10 minutes, and then reduce heat to 300 degrees F and bake another 50 minutes until cake has risen but center still jiggles. Remove from oven; cool at room temperature for 15 minutes, then chill until ready to serve. (This can be made a day or two ahead and it often tastes better this way. Or freeze until ready to remove the outer ring.)

In a small saucepan, heat the curd to just warm. In a bowl, mix the water and cornstarch and whisk into the curd. Add the lemon zest. Cook over low heat for 3 to 4 minutes, whisking often until thickened and smooth; cool slightly. Pour over the cheesecake when the cake has chilled and the glaze is at room temperature. Chill until ready to serve. Garnish with a strawberry, pansy, or mint sprig (or all three!).
Each cake serves 6.

lemon ricotta cakes with fruit

Lusciously light and lemony, these little cakes provide all the
flavor of lemon and fruit of the season in one bite.

Special equipment:
    ten 6-ounce decorative
    metal molds or two
    6-inch-round cake pans

1 cup sugar

1 cup unsalted butter, softened

1 cup whole milk ricotta cheese

$\frac{1}{2}$ cup whole milk

3 cups all-purpose flour

$\frac{1}{2}$ teaspoon baking powder

Finely grated zest of
    1 large lemon

Juice of 1 lemon

4 large eggs

TOPPING

3 cups blueberries,
    sliced strawberries,
    raspberries, or peaches

$\frac{1}{2}$ cup sugar

1 teaspoon lemon juice

Powdered sugar

In the bowl of a mixer, beat together the sugar and
butter until light yellow and fluffy, about 2 minutes
on medium speed. Add the ricotta, milk, flour,
baking powder, lemon zest, lemon juice, and eggs
and beat well for 2 minutes on medium speed.

Spray the molds or cake pans with vegetable oil or
nonstick cooking spray. Place $\frac{1}{2}$ cup batter into each
mold, spreading tops evenly, or divide the batter
between the cake pans. Bake the molds at 350 degrees
F on a baking sheet for 25 minutes, or the cake pans
for 45 minutes, or until a toothpick inserted in the
center comes out clean. Cool cakes.

To prepare the topping, in a medium bowl
combine the fruit, sugar, and lemon juice. Serve
an individual cake or a small slice of cake with
a spoonful of fruit topping on top. Dust with
powdered sugar. *Serves 10.*

momma's italian apple cake

My mother loved to bake. She wrote out all her recipes, longhand, and
secured them with straight pins. No staples for her. And all her beating
was done by hand with a handheld mixer. Chopping was done only
with knives on a wooden board. No food processor, no Kitchen-Aid.
A purist. And a perfectionist. Here is one of her favorite fall desserts.
It's perfect served with a cup of espresso with a twist of lemon.

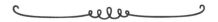

½ cup unsalted butter,
    softened

½ cup sugar

4 egg yolks, room
   temperature

½ teaspoon finely grated
   lemon zest

2 cups all-purpose flour

2 teaspoons baking powder

4 egg whites, room
   temperature

3 large Granny Smith
   apples, peeled, cored,
   and thinly sliced

   Powdered sugar

In the bowl of a mixer, beat the butter and sugar until
light yellow and fluffy, about 2 minutes on medium
speed. Add the egg yolks, lemon zest, flour, and
baking powder. The batter will be very stiff.

Beat the egg whites until stiff peaks form. Fold the egg
whites into the batter. Again, the batter will be stiff.
Add the sliced apples to the batter.

Spread the batter into a 9-inch cake pan that has
been sprayed with vegetable oil or nonstick cooking
spray. Bake on the middle rack of a preheated
450-degree-F oven for 15 minutes, and then
reduce heat to 375 degrees F and bake an additional
25 minutes. Remove from oven and cool for at least
30 minutes before slicing. Serve sprinkled with
powdered sugar. *Serves 8 to 10*.

spiced mini carrot cake cupcakes

Moist mini carrot cake cupcakes are a perfect party finger food. Crowned with a cream cheese frosting, each morsel will be a bite of carrot cake perfection.

1 large orange (use Cara Cara oranges if in season)

2 cups all-purpose flour

3/4 cup sugar

2 teaspoons baking powder

2 teaspoons baking soda

2 teaspoons ground cinnamon

1 teaspoon nutmeg

1/2 teaspoon ground cloves

1/2 teaspoon kosher salt

1 teaspoon vanilla extract

3/4 cup canola oil

4 large eggs

2 cups finely grated carrots

1/2 cup finely chopped nuts (pecans, walnuts, almonds, or macadamia)

1/4 cup liqueur (dark rum, cointreau, or brandy)

CREAM CHEESE FROSTING

16 ounces cream cheese, softened

2 cups powdered sugar

1/2 cup butter, softened

1 teaspoon vanilla extract

Wash orange and cut into 8 wedges. Remove white pith and seeds, if any. Cut into small pieces and puree in a blender or food processor; set aside.

In the bowl of a mixer, combine the flour, sugar, baking powder, baking soda, cinnamon, nutmeg, cloves, and salt. Beat in the vanilla, oil, orange puree, eggs, carrots, nuts, and liqueur until well blended. Pour the batter into mini muffin tins lined with mini paper cups (batter makes enough for about 56 mini cupcakes). Fill the muffin cups almost all the way to the top. Bake on the middle rack of a preheated 350-degree-F oven for 15 minutes; cool completely.

Beat the cream cheese, powdered sugar, butter, and vanilla until smooth. Pipe the frosting on each cupcake using a plastic disposable pastry tube or a plastic ziplock bag with the tip cut off. *Makes about 56 mini cupcakes.*

NOTE: If desired, add food coloring to the cream cheese frosting as you are beating the ingredients.

Index

Metric Conversion Chart

Volume Measurements

U.S.	Metric
1 teaspoon	5 ml
1 tablespoon	15 ml
1/4 cup	60 ml
1/3 cup	75 ml
1/2 cup	125 ml
2/3 cup	150 ml
3/4 cup	175 ml
1 cup	250 ml

Weight Measurements

U.S.	Metric
1/2 ounce	15 g
1 ounce	30 g
3 ounces	90 g
4 ounces	115 g
8 ounces	225 g
12 ounces	350 g
1 pound	450 g
2 1/4 pounds	1 kg

Temperature Conversion

Fahrenheit	Celsius
250	120
300	150
325	160
350	180
375	190
400	200
425	220
450	230